FONT OF LIFE

ALSO BY GARRY WILLS

FONT *of* LIFE

AMBROSE, AUGUSTINE, AND THE
MYSTERY OF BAPTISM

GARRY WILLS

OXFORD
UNIVERSITY PRESS

OXFORD
UNIVERSITY PRESS

Oxford University Press, Inc., publishes works that further
Oxford University's objective of excellence
in research, scholarship, and education.

Oxford   New York
Auckland   Cape Town   Dar es Salaam   Hong Kong   Karachi
Kuala Lumpur   Madrid   Melbourne   Mexico City   Nairobi
New Delhi   Shanghai   Taipei   Toronto

With offices in
Argentina   Austria   Brazil   Chile   Czech Republic   France   Greece
Guatemala   Hungary   Italy   Japan   Poland   Portugal   Singapore
South Korea   Switzerland   Thailand   Turkey   Ukraine   Vietnam

Copyright © 2012 by Garry Wills

Published by Oxford University Press, Inc.
198 Madison Avenue, New York, New York 10016

www.oup.com

Oxford is a registered trademark of Oxford University Press

Library of Congress Cataloging-in-Publication Data
Wills, Garry, 1934–
Font of life : Ambrose, Augustine and the mystery of baptism / Garry Wills.
p. cm. — (Emblems of antiquity)
Includes bibliographical references and index.
ISBN 978-0-19-976851-6
1. Ambrose, Saint, Bishop of Milan, d. 397. 2. Augustine, Saint, Bishop of Hippo.
3. Milan (Italy)—Church history. I. Title.
BR1720.A9W54 2012
270.2092′51—dc23
[B]
2011026828

1 3 5 7 9 8 6 4 2

Printed in the United States of America
on acid-free paper

TO NATALIE

with whom I spent fascinating weeks exploring all the Ambrosian churches in and around ancient Milan

Contents

Acknowledgments

———————

I am deeply grateful to those who read the whole book and offered valuable suggestions—James J. O'Donnell, Glen Bowersock, Harold Drake, and (my editor) Stefan Vranka. As usual, my wife, Natalie, corrected and improved what I wrote, and my agent, Andrew Wylie, had my back.

Key to Brief Citations

B   Peter Brown, *Religion and Society in the Age of Saint Augustine* (Harper & Row, 1972)

C   Augustine, *Confessions*, translated by Garry Wills (Penguin, 2006)

CCL   Corpus Christianorum, Series Latina (Brepols, 1953–)

CSEL   *Corpus Scriptorum Ecclesiasticorum Latinorum* (Johnson Reprint Corporation, 1962)

Epistulae Ambrose, *Epistulae* (CSEL 82. 1, 2, 4); Augustine, *Epistulae* (CSEL 34, 44, 57)

G   Josef Schmitz, *Gottesdienst im altchristlichen Mailand* (Peter Hanstein Verlag, 1975)

LP	Alan Cameron, *The Last Pagans of Rome* (Oxford University Press, 2011)
M	Ambrose, *De Mysteriis*
O	Ambrose, *De Officiis*, trans. and ed. Ivor J. Davidson (Oxford University Press, 2001)
P	Paulinus, *Vita Ambrosii*
PL	*Patrologia Latina* (Congregatio Sancti Mauri, 1844–)
S	Ambrose, *De Sacramentis* (CSEL 73, Part 7)
U	Uncollected letters of Ambrose (*Epistulae Extra Collectionem*, CSEL 82, Part 4)
V	Ambrose, *De Virginibus*

All translations are by the author, except for those from Hebrew, where the New English Bible is used.

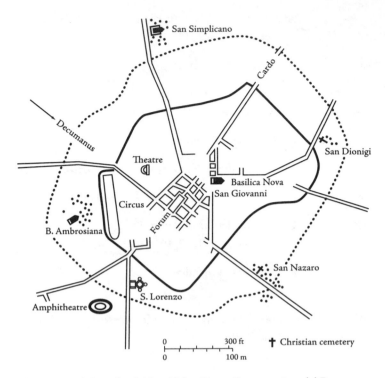

The Episcopal Complex, Milan. (After Piazza Duomo prima del Duomo, a cura di S. Lusuardi Siena, Milano 2009, p. 5.)

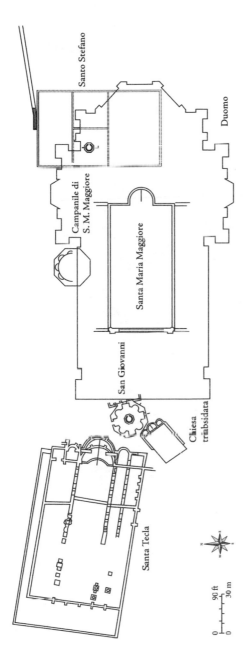

Ambrose's cathedral complex, archaeological remains with an overlay of the later Duomo. (San Giovanni was the medieval name of Ambrose's baptistry.)

FONT OF LIFE

———

TALE OF A FONT

There is a certain romance to archeology, the dream of delving downward to bring up a lost world. Heinrich Schliemann pursued the romance of resurrecting the Troy of Priam and the Mycenae of Agamemnon. The romance continues. I did not appreciate the power of polychrome marble buildings in Greece till I went down into the tumulus at Vergina and saw the still-fresh colors on the Macedonian tomb building there. But one of the most emotionally charged underground sites I have encountered is that of a sunken cathedral and baptistry under the piazza of the Milan Cathedral (the Duomo).

Few people go down under the smooth and trafficked surface of the piazza. For a favorite tourist view they go up to the roof of the Duomo, where they walk between towering forests of spires and statues to gaze out at the Alps. Modern visitors can ride an elevator to that height, but in the past many tourists (including Alfred, Lord Tennyson) climbed 158 stairs to get there. In Luchino Visconti's 1960 film *Rocco and His Brothers*, a key scene takes place

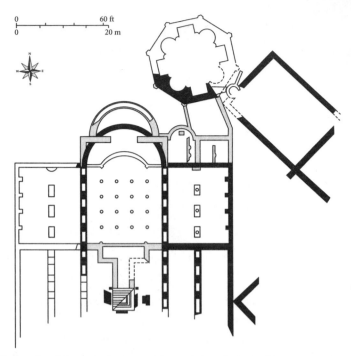

Figure I.1 The find of 1941–43. From A. De Capitani d'Arzago, *La chiesa maggiore di Milano: Santa Tecla* (Ceschina, 1952), pl. 2.

on the Duomo roof. In a misguided attempt at saintliness, Rocco (Alain Delon) tells the woman who loves him that she must go back to the man who raped her, since that man needs her more than he does. The talk is ironically placed against the throng of saintly and angelic figures on the roof, with views down toward the tiny people below, as Rocco attempts an otherworldliness that shrinks the woman. We last see her as the camera gazes down at her running the whole length of the cathedral roof, hounded by a blighting virtue.

To enter a world of real saintliness, we must go down from the airy heights of the Duomo, which Mark Twain called "a fairy delusion of frost-work," descending even lower than the dwarfed

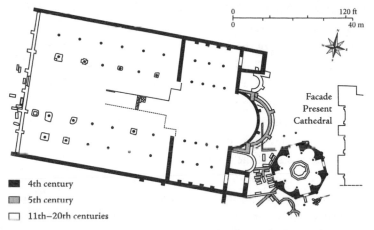

Figure I.2 The finds of 1961–63. From Richard Krautheimer and Slobodan Ćurčić, *Early Christian and Byzantine Architecture*, 4th ed. (Yale University Press, 1986), p. 84.

people seen from above in the piazza, and enter a dark underworld of stones arranged in patterns long forgotten. These foundations were discovered by accident as men dug for a bomb shelter under the piazza in World War II. The haste of completing the refuge did not allow for thorough excavation of the find—only part of a basilica was revealed, along with two sides of an eight-walled building beside it, presumed to be the baptistry (fig. I.1). The discoverer of this treasure, Alberto De Capitani d'Arzago, died in 1948 before he could write up his final report on the dig.

It had long been suspected that there were structures under the piazza. Stones were discovered in 1870 while a drainage pipe was being laid. In 1914 Ugo Monneret de Villard made an educated guess that they belonged to the Basilica Nova, which the bishop of Milan, Ambrose, had described during his time as its pastor (374–97). After this was confirmed in the wartime dig, further exploration occurred in 1961–63, as a side effect of constructing the metropolitan subway system. The archeology of this project was conducted by Mario Mirabella Roberti, the superintendent of antiquities of Lombardy, who turned up foundations of the whole Basilica Nova and of the separate baptistry building (Figure I.2).[1]

The basilica (called in medieval times Santa Tecla) is huge, with a five-aisled nave, and lateral chambers to its apse. It is 269 feet long (88 yards, almost as long as a football field) and 148 feet wide. It could hold as many as three thousand people, almost as many as the pope's contemporary church in Rome, the Lateran Basilica.[2] It was built toward the middle of the fourth century, perhaps during the time of Bishop Auxentius (355–74). The marble bases of the church's columns are surmounted by the beginnings of polychrome shafts. Traces of frescos are on the surviving lower sections of wall. All these things testify to the prosperity of the church in Milan even before Ambrose presided there. Maria Teresa Fiorio writes: "Its exceptionally large scale puts Santa Tecla among the most imposing basilicas for that time in the West, fitting the imperial dignity attained by Milan. Its plan resembled eastern types like the Christian basilicas of Greece—but it provides an example preceding those of Dodona, Epidaurus, or Thebes, which date from as late as the fifth century" (F 50).

An octagonal baptistry building—62 feet wide, from corner to corner—stands beside the basilica. The workmanship is of the same high quality as that of the basilica. Inside the building is an octagonal pool for baptizing by total immersion. It is twenty feet across (from corner to corner) and two and a half feet deep to the level of its current brim.[3] It is very likely the place where Ambrose was baptized in 374 (he had been elected bishop before he was ordained a priest, or even baptized). It is more certainly the place where Ambrose baptized Augustine in 387.

This octagonal baptistry was the most sacred place in fourth-century Milan. Ambrose called it "the holy of holies" (M 5). He compared it to the inner tabernacle of the Temple in Jerusalem, which the high priest could enter once a year (S 4.1–2), since only the ministers and recipients of baptism could see the inside of the baptistry, and only on Easter. Ambrose wove around the building and its rituals an elaborate web of symbolism, which made it the model for later baptistries throughout the north of Italy and the south of France. This was not only because of his own and Augustine's baptism there; it is also because the rite of baptism was central to Christian life at the time. It took place for all those joining the church only once a year, and it came at the climax of the liturgical year, on Easter morning, the spring celebration of rebirth. It was a communal event, not a private one. It was preceded and followed by intense instruction of the new Christians, who wore distinctive insignia and were set apart from the rest of the congregation, first as penitents, then as triumphal beginners of a new life.

The baptistry building was itself a link between the old and new. The baptizands went out from the Basilica Vetus (Old Basilica), also known as the Ecclesia Hiemalis, where the liturgy had been celebrated during the winter seasons of Advent and Lent, and—after their baptism—they led the whole community into the Basilica Nova (New Basilica), the Ecclesia Aestiva, where the glorious feasts would be held (Easter, Ascension, Pentecost) in the birth of a new year.[1] The newly baptized, who led the procession into the new basilica, were clothed in white "garments of paradise," which made Ambrose greet them with the cry from the Song of Songs (8.5): "What cohort comes up from the desert all in white?" (S 4.5, M 35–39, G 22–23; "all in white" reflects Ambrose's Latin biblical text). Ambrose preached that baptism had a symbolic "type" in the passage of Israelites through the Red Sea (S 12). It was also prefigured in the Passover. So the literal passing over from the Basilica Vetus to the Basilica Nova was a dramatic enactment of the meaning of baptism.

The process of baptism at that time gave Christians who underwent it the deepest spiritual experience they would ever have. Peter Brown rightly calls it "this drastic rite" (B 201). For all forty days of Lent the candidates engaged in fasts and penance.

They were instructed twice a day by the bishop himself, and once a week they underwent a physical inspection (*scrutamen*) that was part of the exorcism function of baptism, to free them from diabolical interference with their bodies.[5] A week before baptism, they were for the first time entrusted with the creed, which they had to memorize without writing it down. It was to guard them as "a constant protection and keepsake of [their] hearts."[6]

Before dawn in 387, Augustine and his fellows gathered at the entrance to the baptistry, where Ambrose performed a ceremony of opening (Effetha) by touching their ears and nostrils, so they would have a heightened spiritual awareness of what they were about to see and do. Then, just inside the baptistry, they faced west and renounced the devil, before facing east and welcoming the coming of Christ into their hearts. After this, they stripped off their clothes in one of the building's recesses, before being anointed with oil all over their bodies "like athletes" (S 1.2, G 105–6). Then they stepped down into the baptismal pool, escorted by the bishop and his deacon, who ducked each person's head under the water three times as they professed belief in each member of the Trinity. As they came out of the pool, they were wrapped in a white garment signifying their innocence. They were anointed again, though this time only on the head. After that, the bishop washed their feet—a last gesture of exorcism, since the serpent in Eden had bitten Adam in the foot (S 3.5)—then they received a "seal of the Spirit" and went to the New Basilica. For the first time, they heard the Lord's Prayer and participated in the Eucharist.

To appreciate the sacred drama that took place there, we have to rebuild in our mind Milan's baptistry from the foundational traces revealed by modern archeology.[7] The most salient fact about the shape of the building is its eight sides, a multivalent symbol Ambrose explains in great detail. The single-center building imitates the mausoleums of the time. Ambrose emphasizes that "it looks like a tomb." But in the imperial mausoleums familiar to people in Milan, bodies were deposited to lie in death. In the baptistry, a death was to be reenacted, as believers died into Christ beneath the waters of the font, but this death was followed by a resurrection, as they rose into Christ and entered into eternal life. As Paul wrote (Romans 6.4): "All we baptized into Messiah Jesus were baptized into his death. We were buried with him by virtue of this death-by-baptism, so that, just as Messiah rose from the dead in the splendor of the Father, so we shall fare on with renewed life."

The number eight was a symbol of eternity, since it followed on the seven days of creation in the Bible and it was the number for Sunday, the day of Christ's Resurrection. Ambrose often emphasized this sacred meaning: "The seventh day revealed the mystery of the Law; the eighth day revealed the mystery of the Resurrection."[8]

> The seventh day belongs to the Old Testament; the eighth belongs to the New, when Christ rose from the dead, and the light of a new form of salvation penetrated us all. This day the prophet referred to when he said, "This is the day the Lord made, let us rejoice and be glad in it" (Psalms 118.24). On this day the brilliance of the entire and completed circumcision flooded in on sinners. For the Old Testament gave a partial meaning to the day in the rite of circumcision—though that was still veiled in a shadow. Now the sun of Justice arrives and, by the completion of his own suffering, beams out his rays of illumination. He unveiled the sun to all and broke open the incandescence of eternal life.[9]

Baptism was a new beginning in a setting of new beginnings—at dawn (the beginning of day), in spring (the beginning of the year), on Easter (the beginning of salvation). Ambrose even thought that Easter occurred on the exact anniversary of the first day of creation (the vernal equinox). His warrant for this was Exodus 12.2: "This month shall be for you the beginning of months."

What is called the Pasch of the Lord is celebrated at the beginning of spring. In this beginning of the months he made the heavens and the earth, which was when the world first arose. This season of warmth favors all things, and it bears the appearance of a world coming to birth, of a calm and warm sun shining out after the ice and darknesses of winter.[10]

Within the eight walls, the floor of the baptistry is inlaid with elegant intarsia work of varying black and white marble tesserae (mosaic tiles) in three different patterns. There are eight niches in the walls, alternating rectangular shapes and semicircular apse recesses. There are entries through the outer wall at each rectangle. The niches were presumably used for unclothing and reclothing the baptizands before and after their immersion in the pool. The bases of eight columns are spaced about the inner circuit formed by the projections from each niche. Two columns flank each niche. Mirabella Roberti argues that these columns would have been engaged with the walls, as in the mausoleum at the Basilica Portiana in San Lorenzo (now the Chapel of Saint Aquilino). But Dale Kinney thinks they would have been weight bearing, going all the way up to the cupola that was traditional in such centrally organized mausoleums or chapels.[11] This indicates the building's height, and accords with Ambrose's poem inscribed in the building's interior, which calls the baptistry a "temple raised up . . . to tower" (templum surrexit . . . surgere). For a hypothetical reconstruction of the baptistry, see Remo Rachini's drawing (fig. I.3).[12]

The walls would have held a cupola with a mosaic lining, as in similar mausoleums. Tesserae fallen from it were found on the baptistry floor and in the font, but it is impossible to tell what the design was in the fourth century, since a medieval replacement of it has also shed tesserae. The high walls of the interior would have had a row of windows around the upper level, as in the mausoleums on which it is patterned. The doors closed for the ceremony

Figure I.3 Sketch of probable baptistry. From Silvia Lusuardi Siena, ed., *Piazza Duomo prima del Duomo*, (Veneranda Fabbrica del Duomo di Milano, 2009); drawing by Remo Rachini, courtesy of Istituto di Archeologia, Università Cattolica del Sacro Cuore.

would have left the building dim below and glowing above. There were probably mosaic or fresco designs on the walls, and I shall address later whether we can make an informed guess about their content from Ambrose's words inside the baptistry.

The poem Ambrose dedicated to the building is preserved in a copy made by an eighth-century pilgrim and recopied in the ninth or tenth century on a Vatican manuscript (Palatine Codex 833). Where the eight elegiac distichs of the Latin poem were inscribed in the building must be a matter of conjecture (G 11–12). But it is reasonable to suppose that they were put, one to a wall, just below the line of windows, where they would be most legible. There is a whole theology of baptism in the poem.[13]

Octachorum sanctos templum surrexit in usus
Octagonus fons est munere dignus eo.
[This eight-niched temple has risen to holy purpose,
And eight sides of the font perform their task.]
Hoc numero decuit sacri baptismatis aulam
Surgere quo populis vera salus rediit.
[That number befits a chamber for baptizing,
It towers so that people may be saved.]
Luce resurgentis Christi qui claustra resolvit
Mortis et tumulis suscitat examines.
[In the splendor of Christ's rising, to break the bars
Of death and bring life out of tombs.]
Confessosque reos maculoso crimine solvens
Fontis puriflui diluit inriguo.
[Freeing from sin's stain repenting men,
Cleansed in the font's pure-running stream.]
Hic quicumque volunt probrosa crimina vitae
Ponere corda lavent pectora munda gerant.
[Here those shedding vile crimes of their past
 May wash their hearts and take away pure breasts.]
Huc veniant alacres quamvis tenebrosus adire
Audeat, abscedet candidior nivibus
[Here let them swiftly come. Here anyone who dares,
However darkened, will go off whiter than snow.]

Huc sancti properent non expers ullus aquarum
Sanctus, in his regnum est consiliumque Dei.
[Let saints run here, since no one can be saintly
Without these waters, by God's reign and plan.]
Gloria justitiae nam quid divinius isto
Ut puncto exiguo culpa cadat populi?
[Here flares the right. What can be more God's work
Than removing sin in an eyeblink?]

The poem spells out what the baptizands underwent as they died into the water, rose reanimated from it, and were "clothed in Christ." The font is fed with water from four spouts on the axial sides of the pool, signifying the four rivers of paradise (Genesis 2.11–14) (fig. I.4). There is only one drain, and it provides for running water in the pool, symbolizing the "living water" from the ceaseless font of eternal life (John 4.14). The early liturgical book *Didache* (7.1) shows the importance of baptism in "living water,"

Figure I.4 The baptismal pool. Courtesy Art History Images.

and Ambrose's poem speaks of sinners "cleansed in the font's pure-running stream" (fontis periflui diluit inriguo). The pool is two and a half feet deep to its present top, but for total immersion the sides must have been higher before their upper part was razed in the six-teenth century for the paving of the piazza to the modern Duomo.

This is the font the thirty-three-year-old Augustine entered at dawn on April 25 in 387, to be baptized by the forty-eight-year-old Ambrose. Augustine was accompanied by his sixteen-year-old son Adeodatus and his best friend and coeval, Alypius. The three of them were joined by others seeking baptism, after Ambrose's intense and long preparation of them for this moment. The ceremony was especially dramatic in 387 because, among other things, it marked the first anniversary of Ambrose's most emotional conflict with his imperial opponents and their heretical allies. On Easter 386, while Ambrose was involved in his time-consuming baptismal duties, Emperor Valentinian II and his regent mother, Justina, tried to seize by force the Basilica Nova, into which Ambrose was about to lead his newly baptized members. Ambrose fought back with emotional services around the clock in the Basilica Vetus, next door to the occupied church, keeping the congregation awake and involved with new forms of antiphonal chant, "ready to die with their bishop" (C 9.15). Augustine's mother was a fervent participant in these acts of defiance, though Augustine was still keeping a cool distance from them (something he now regretted as he approached the font at one of the contested basilicas).

This was, indeed, the first Easter in three years that passed without some menace from and struggle with Valentinian's court (the court to which Augustine had been attached as official or-ator until a few months before he enrolled for baptism). There was an element of triumphal celebration in this year's Easter rites, which Augustine found so moving that he remembered ever after his feelings when the Ambrosian congregation lifted its old holy battle songs while Augustine went to the altar for his first

Eucharist: "How many tears I wept at your hymns and canticles, abruptly carried away by the sweetly tuned voices of your church. The voices flowed in at my ears, your truth distilled in my heart, a wash of emotion arose in me" (C 9.14). In the week after they were baptized, Ambrose explained to the new Christians things previously kept under the *disciplina arcani* (religious secrets). This probably brought them back to the baptistry, as Ambrose expounded what had happened there.

The weeks of baptismal instruction Augustine received twice daily from Ambrose were of crucial importance to him. It was his most prolonged and convincing exposure to Ambrose's method of using the Jewish scripture in typological senses, as prefigurements of the revelation complete in Jesus. This at last cleared up a long-standing problem Augustine had with the older parts of the Bible, which he had considered a primitive muddle, just as the Manicheans taught him (C 3.9–10). Much of the medieval approach to the Bible as allegory would develop from this cross-fertilization of the minds of Ambrose and Augustine on the subject of biblical typology.

Indeed, much of medieval Christendom in the West acquired its broad contours from what took place here. The church would learn to act according to Ambrose's ruling patterns—his development of doctrinal rigor (especially on the Nicene Creed), the centrality of baptism, liturgical expansiveness, monastic discipline, the cult of saints, and episcopal control. And the church would learn to think with the imaginative flights and intellectual daring of Augustine. All this important history is foreshadowed in the events of that Easter morning at the font. And the drama lurks, if we just attend to it, in the various stones turned up in 1943 while Milan's people were trying to duck Allied bombs near their Duomo.

Yet my wife and I were sometimes alone, or joined at other times only by two or three others, in that underground baptistry.

The entrance to it, just inside the main entrance to the Duomo, is unobtrusive, a narrow stairway with a modest sign:

INGRESSO e 4.00
BATTISTERO PALAEOCHRISTIANO
ORARI 9:30–17.30

The few who go down stand in strong contrast to the line formed at the other end of the Duomo for the *ascensore* taking them up to the roof of the church, which is a teeming tourist site on this largest Gothic cathedral in Europe—one built, incongruously, of classical white marble. Its exterior has 135 spires and 1,156 brackets, to hold 2,326 statues, many of which cluster on the roof.[14] From that high vantage point, on a clear day, there are long views of Lombard geography. But those who go down to the hidden treasure under all this white extravaganza can, with a little imagination, see even longer vistas of history in the making. Everything that happened in that vast structure above, though it took place partly under the abiding sway of Ambrose, was less spiritually important than what happened here below.

PART I

MILAN

AMBROSE'S TOWN

M ilan bears the mark of Ambrose, even sixteen centuries after his death. He was Milan's bishop from 374 to 397 CE, and the ring of churches he created or took over continues to exist in some form. Many things associated with Milan still bear his name—Ambrosian chant, Ambrosian hymns, the Ambrosian Rite (*Ambrosianum Mysterium*),[1] the Ambrosian School (*Scientia Ambrosiana*),[2] Ambrosian singers, the Ambrosian Choir, the Ambrosian Library, the Ambrosian Bank, the Ambrosian Picture Gallery (*Pinacoteca*), Ambrosian this and Ambrosian that. Down through the centuries streets and shops and little boys were named for Ambrose—the sixteenth-century Milanese artists Ambrogio Bergognone and Ambrogio Figina both painted their namesake. Local tortellini are called *Raviolata d'Ambrogio*. The city's famous opera house, La Scala, begins its season every year on Ambrose's feast day, December 7, and dedicates its performance to his memory, followed by a banquet paid for by the city, where prizes are awarded in the form of coins incised with a "little Ambrose in gold" (*ambrogino d'oro*).[3]

For days around his feast, much of the town quits work and goes to fairs held around the Castello Sforzesco. If you go inside the Castello, a colossal image of Ambrose rises high above you in the official banner of the city, the Gonfalone d'Ambrogio, a silk tapestry with gold threads displaying the saint's entry into the city through an arch of triumph (fig. 1.1). Blessed by Archbishop Charles Borromeo in 1566, the pendant flag is too large to be borne by men. It led processions on a special wheeled carriage, with strut wires to keep it upright.

But Ambrosian memories in the later history of Milan are nothing compared to the hold he had on the place in his lifetime. He clashed with three Roman emperors—Gratian, Valentinian II, and Theodosius—who often lived across town from him; and he prevailed in all three conflicts. As the distinguished historian of late antiquity J. H. W. G. Liebeschuetz writes: "In the whole of Roman history, few if any individuals confronted emperors in the way Ambrose did repeatedly. . . . Whatever we think of the causes he took up, nobody can question that he always displayed exemplary courage, both moral and physical."[4] Even the acerbically secular Edward Gibbon saluted Ambrose, as it were, across a theological barricade:

> The palm of episcopal vigor and ability was justly claimed
> by the intrepid Ambrose. . . . He condescended, for the
> good of the church, to direct the conscience of the em-
> perors and to control the administration of the empire. . . .
> He exercised, with equal firmness and dexterity, the power
> of his spiritual and political characters.[5]

Gibbon's treatment of Ambrose so impressed Richard Wagner that he thought plays or operas should be written about the bishop.[6] As Ambrose himself put it, "You yourselves know that ordinarily I defer to emperors but do not truckle to them" ("soleam deferre non cedere," *Letters* 75A.2).

Figure 1.1 Gonfalone d'Ambrogio. Courtesy Castello Sforzesco,
© Comune di Milano—all rights reserved.

In the fourth century, Milan was the omphalos of the Western
Roman Empire, and Ambrose did not let the imperial court out-
shine his ecclesiastical domain. Rome was no longer the center of the
empire. Challenges from northern peoples made it necessary for the

Western emperor to be closer to the military action of the time, and he used three different capitals—Trier when the threat seemed imminent on the Rhine, Sirmium when it was coming from the Danube, and Milan as a middle point, a staging area between the other two, and the court's favored base during Ambrose's years in Milan.

Ambrose was determined to create a spiritual identity for his city, over which he had once ruled as its secular governor. He started out with a certain topographical advantage when he became the city's bishop. The double cathedral he inherited—a complex containing the Basilica Vetus and adjacent Basilica Nova—was central to the city's population as it had grown in the preceding years. The former center, in the west of town, was near the forum of Roman Mediolanum, situated as usual where the axial Roman roads (*decumanus* and *cardo*) met. There the imperial palace was located, near the circus racetrack and the theater for drama, and (just outside the walls) the arena for games. Just outside the Porta was the Basilica Portiana (later San Lorenzo) over which Ambrose and the emperor Valentinian would contend for ownership.

In the eastern part of town, more densely populated and "modern," Ambrose's twin churches were buffered by the homes and shops of his congregation. When in 385–86, the anti-Nicene (Arian) emperor tried to kidnap Ambrose and expel him from town (P 12), his soldiers had to go through crowds rallying around Ambrose and his church, where Ambrose was popular for his benefactions to the poor and his fervent inculcation of the Nicene (Trinitarian) faith. And when the emperor tried to seize the Basilica Nova, on Ambrose's side of town, the bishop's loyal people flooded the area and baffled the attempted occupation. Augustine, the African saint, was in Milan at the time, working for the emperor and presumably living at or near the court. He saw the flux and reflux of crowds through the city's streets and was "shaken by the turbulence rocking the city" (C 9.15). He witnessed the power of Ambrose in its supreme test, and for a while considered him a demagogue.

But Ambrose, during his reign over the city, did not settle for command in the city's dense neighborhoods and crowded streets. He created or commandeered four or five tall and imposing churches in a ring outside the city walls, closely linking them to his urban center by processions and seasonal celebrations. No matter how one came at the city, on major roads from Rome or Trier or Sirmium or Pavia, one encountered these outposts and sentries of the church system Ambrose maintained. Power emanated from the center, circulated through these outlying bastions, and returned to its source. On the north, by the road to the imperial capital of Trier, was the Basilica Virginum (now San Simpliciano).[7] On the southeast, along the road to Rome, just outside the most formal gate into the city, was the Basilica Apostolorum (now San Nazaro).[8] To the southwest, hemming in the southern part of the imperial quarters, was the Basilica Portiana (now San Lorenzo), with a separate mausoleum (now Sant'Aquilino).[9] To the west, skirting the central part of the imperial quarters, was the Basilica Martyrum (now Sant'Ambrogio), with its separate mausoleum (San Vittore).[10] And (perhaps) to the northeast, by the road to Aquileia, and thence to the imperial capital at Sirmium, was the Basilica Prophetarum (later San Dionigi).[11]

The most important motive in raising these suburban churches may not seem obvious now. Ambrose was faced with the fact that some of these spaces were already sacred, and could become rivals to his urban institutions. Christians had followed the old pagan custom of burying their dead outside the city walls, and Christian martyrs in these cemeteries were soon honored with shrines (martyria) which acquired cult followings. Women especially were the devotees at these shrines. Ambrose had to block Augustine's mother, Monnica,[12] from bringing African practices to a Milan martyrium (C 6.2).

> For women in the ancient world, the cemetery areas had
> always been a zone of "low gravity," where their movements

and choice of company were less subject to male scrutiny and the control of the family. The new shrines, when not crowded on days of festival, were oases of peace and beauty, with flowing water and rustling trees, filled with the cooing of white doves.[13]

The spontaneity and fervor of these pious exercises made them potential rivals of the ceremonies of the official clergy. This challenge from the periphery resembles the popularity of the desert fathers in the Eastern church, which tended to undermine the authority of bishop and priest. In response to this competition, Athanasius in Alexandria insisted that the regular clergy should adopt some of the ascetical practices of the hermits (including celibacy) to restore his men's standing with the people.[14]

The rock-star celebrity of martyrs in the early church is hard to exaggerate.[15] Their shrines were to be found throughout North Italy.[16] Martyrs were so admired that even the pagan historian Ammianus Marcellinus showed respect for them.[17] The emperors whose reigns Ammianus recorded were themselves ardent acquirers and celebrants of martyr relics, sometimes to the discomfort of bishops trying to restrain these rival centers of religiosity.[18] In the early *Martyrdom of Polycarp* it was said that martyr relics were "more precious than rare jewels or than gold." Ambrose, in order to assert his authority over the martyr shrines, gave them a new focus, raising his own churches in these already sanctified spaces, binding them into a single discipline. What might seem at first glance a dispersal of power was actually a way of consolidating it. He turned centrifugal energies into centripetal ones. Or, in Peter Brown's more elegant image, Ambrose "was like an electrician who rewires an antiquated wiring system; more power could pass through stronger, better-insulated wires toward the bishop as leader of the community."[19] To keep the system united, Ambrose orchestrated seasonal celebrations at these various stations, conducting pilgrimages around them while maintaining the central source of this activity.[20] Even when his own city church was under siege, he kept up his daily processions to the martyria (*Epistulae* 76).

Ambrose knew that control of the martyr cult was essential to control of his people. He often expressed his own desire to suffer a martyr's death. He praised his brother and sister as virtual martyrs, appropriately buried next to martyrs as he would be when he died.[21] He braced his congregation for possible martyrdom when his church was besieged by the emperor's troops, and he praised martyrs of the Old Testament (the Maccabees) before his candidates for baptism. The crowning triumph of his struggle with Emperor Valentinian II and his regent mother Justina was his discovery of the bodies of the martyred twins Gervase and Protase at the suburban shrine to Milanese saints, and the subsequent miracles performed by the sacred relics. Ambrose became known as a champion finder of martyrs' relics (P 14, 29, 32, 52). Alan Cameron notes that Pope Damasus (366–84) made Rome more sacred because he "found and adorned the tombs of scores of martyrs" there (*LP* 350).

The older churches Ambrose took over—the double cathedral downtown and the Basilica Portiana outside the walls—were built in a comparatively leisurely way, with quarried blocks in the foundation, and large Roman-sized bricks over a heavy concrete core. The churches he built himself have smaller bricks in herringbone patterns (*opus spicatum*); they were raised rapidly (though on a grand scale) and at great expense (O 347, 790) as Ambrose worked to consolidate his hold on the scattered energies of the faithful.[22] To the major churches of his dominion, inside and outside the city, should be added other freestanding structures— other churches (including Santa Fausta), baptistries, his episcopal residence (*episcopium*), buildings for his platoons of priests ministering at the various sites, at least one monastery-hermitage in the neighboring countryside (*C* 8.15), new and old shrines, stations for the feeding and care of the poor, lodgings for the virgins who came to Milan to be consecrated by him (*V* 1.57), and (probably) a catechumeneum in which applicants for baptism were taught.

Ambrose tended to the construction and upkeep of all his churches while he was also preaching sermons (twice daily in Lent), writing theological treatises, maintaining a far-flung correspondence, hunting for heretics, promoting Nicene bishops in other places, going on missions to the imperial headquarters at Trier, or organizing councils at home or in Aquileia. His army of scribes, secretaries, and diplomatic agents helped fill the days of his energetic time as bishop. It is no wonder that Augustine, while he was serving as court orator to Emperor Valentinian II, felt neglected when he tried to consult Ambrose on his personal problems. Ambrose had better things to do than listen to the queries of a man who had been a protégé of Manicheans and of the pagan Symmachus in Rome (*C* 6.18). On the other hand, when Augustine became an applicant (*competens*) for baptism, he and his fellows were the objects of the most intense care and instruction. Ambrose's secretary-biographer, Paulinus, says that Ambrose was diligent in performing all these exercises personally, so that five men had to replace him in performing the instruction of *competentes* after his death (*P* 38).

After considering Ambrose's overall church strategy, it is useful to look more carefully at the suburban churches, whose original form can still be seen under their later accretions.

SOUTHWEST: BASILICA PORTIANA (SAN LORENZO)

The first basilica Ambrose fought the emperor for in 386 was outside the city wall and near the imperial palace (*Epistulae*

20.1). There is no other convincing candidate for the site but the present San Lorenzo. But was the present San Lorenzo on that site at the time? The matter is extensively debated. Some think it was built during the long episcopate of the Arian Auxentius (355–374), which would give the Arian emperor Valentinian some claim to it in his dispute with Ambrose of 386.[23] But others would date its construction later. Mirabella Roberti says it might have been built in the time of Auxentius, but he inclines more to a time in the 390s.[24] Enrico Cattaneo and his colleagues place it in the time when Stilicho was defending Emperor Honorius in Italy (398–408)—which would explain the fortresslike towers at the four corners of the church (fig. 1.2).[25] Laura Fieni also assigns the church to Stilicho's period, on the basis of radiocarbon dating of its bricks.[26] But W. Eugene Kleinbauer studied the masonry of all pre-Ambrosian remains in Milan and found that their technique is the same as that of the Basilica on which San Lorenzo is based.[27]

In the foundation of the church and parts of its walls there are bits of classical columns, cornices, and capitals, and tons of fill (six thousand pieces under the chapel of Sant'Ippolito alone). The natural supposition is that such a quantity of rubble from a public building of some pretension likely came from demolition of the nearby arena. But when did this occur? Some say it must have been before the 380s, the date of a short poem on Milan by Ausonius, which mentions the theater and circus but not the arena.[28] Others would date it to the time of Alaric's threat. But Dale Kinney, an expert on the use of classical rubble in later buildings, says that constructing such a grand basilica at an exposed site in a time of danger is unlikely. She dates it to the period when Bishop Auxentius was being favored by the emperors Constantius II (337–61) or Valentinian I (364–75), but certainly before the accession of Ambrose as bishop in 374. She makes the case that this grand church complex came from the time when the emperors were

Figure 1.2 Exterior of Basilica Portiana. Courtesy Alec Hartill and Hartill Art Associates, Inc.

trying to make Milan a capital to rank with Rome or Ravenna, and this was their palace church.[29] Its association with Arianism, she argues, has led to the lack of historical clarity about the basilica's early days, since Auxentius was subjected to a *damnatio memoriae* (Orwell's "memory hole") by orthodox Christians in the succeeding years.

It was certainly built on a grand scale—a tetraconch (four-leaf clover) punctuated by four imposing towers, flanked with three octagonal buildings (one a mausoleum), and approached through a colonnaded propylaeum and atrium (fig. 1.3). Even today, with its later additions and alterations, the architectural historian Richard Krautheimer says of it, "The church is still the most beautiful in Milan and among the most beautiful in the Western world."[30] Already in the sixth century it was being called "a wondrous church that excels almost every building in Italy."[31] It was certainly a church worth fighting over in 386. Its

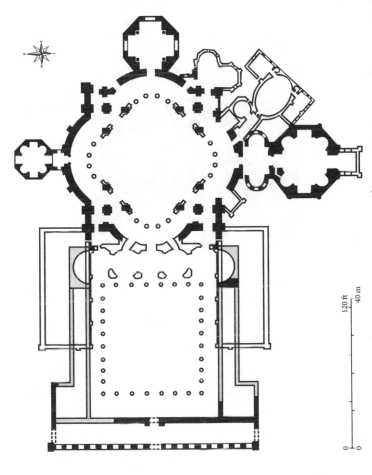

Figure 1.3 Plan of Portiana. From Richard Krautheimer and Slobodan Ćurčić, *Early Christian and Byzantine Architecture*, 4th ed. (Yale University Press, 1986), p.79.

Figure 1.4. Interior of Portiana (© Anthony Scibilia).

grand interior still has the piers of the central structure
(fig. 1.4).[32]

WEST: THE BASILICA MARTYRUM
(SANT'AMBROGIO)

The most important church Ambrose added to the suburbs was
created to absorb the martyr shrine of Milan's patron saints, Nabor
and Felix. These were Roman soldiers thought to have been martyred for the faith in 303, during the persecution of Diocletian.
Their martyrium outside the walls was one of the most sacred
spots when Ambrose became bishop. This was no doubt the place

Monnica was trying to celebrate with gifts of wine and food when Ambrose's sentries prevented her (C 6.2). It was where Ambrose buried his brother, next to the martyrs, since Ambrose felt he was a virtual martyr in his suffering at the threatened invasion of the city.[33] He planned to be buried there himself, and he was.

While constructing the basilica here, Ambrose discovered near the site the bodies of the martyrs Gervase and Protase (P 14). They were supposedly the twin sons of two other Milanese saints. Their father, Vitalis, was martyred under Nero in Ravenna. Their mother, Valeria, was martyred, like her sons, in Milan. Their remains were discovered after Ambrose was informed of their whereabouts in a vision or a dream (Augustine gives accounts of both).[34] A frenzy of devotion, accompanied by a wave of miracles, accompanied the installation of the bodies in Ambrose's new Basilica Martyrum. Augustine was in Milan during this popular celebration, and he reacted to it coolly at the time, though thirteen years later he would join in the adulation when he wrote his *Confessions*.

It is ironic that this church, the only one dedicated to Ambrose, has kept less of its original plan than the others that he raised. This is partly the result of devotion to the saint, leading to endless expansions. It was remade in Carolingian times when Bishop Angilbert (824–59) revived the Ambrosian liturgy and the cult of all "his" martyrs. The most notable mark of this Ambrosian "renaissance" is the altar frontal Angilbert commissioned in 835 from the great metalworker Volvinius. Mirabella Roberti rightly calls it "the most precious work in gold of that era."[35]

In the crypt under the altar is the body of Ambrose, flanked by the bodies of Protase and Gervase. Ambrose's skeleton is dressed in the anachronistic finery of a medieval bishop, though in the church's museum there is a fifth-century mosaic of Ambrose, done seventy years after his death, that has a good

chance of being based on earlier traditions and representations—
and here he wears plain Roman dress, as was common with the
clergy.

SOUTHEAST: BASILICA APOSTOLORUM (SAN NAZARO)

This was built to hold relics of the Apostles Andrew, Thomas, and
John. It was modeled on the Apostoleion in Constantinople, which
had a similar function. The dedicatory poem begins:

> Condidit Ambrosius templum, dominumque sacravit
> Nomine apostolico, munere, reliquiis.
> [Ambrose founded this church, dedicated to the Lord
> With apostolic title, and function, and relics.]

The basilica lay along the road to the Porta Romana, the
entrance to Milan that passed through a triumphal arch, the route of
processions from Rome. Ambrose's dedicatory poem asserts that the
true triumph is that of the cross, marked by the cruciform structure
of the church, a novelty in the West (fig. 1.5). The poem continues:

> Forma crucis templum est, templum victoria Christi,
> Sacra triumphalis signat imago locum.
> [The church has a cross shape, for the conquest of Christ,
> The conquering image is a sign in this place.]

The insistence on the cross as a *sign* of *conquest* draws on
Eusebius's account of Constantine's conquest of Maxentius, the
vision of the cross in the sky, strengthened by a dream, telling him
En touto(i) nika, "In this [sign] conquer!"[36]
We are used to cruciform churches now, but the earlier ones in
Milan and elsewhere had triple, and even quintuple naves, without

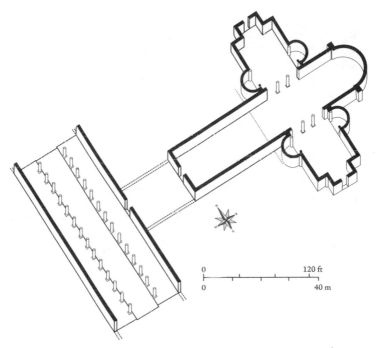

Figure 1.5. Plan of Basilica Apostolorum. From Krautheimer and Ćurčić, *Early Christian and Byzantine Architecture*, p. 82.

pronounced transepts. In the 330s Constantine built the Apostoleion's single nave with a strong crossbar to emphasize the sign of
the cross he had conquered with. This did not have much effect for
the next fifty years. But in the 380s, according to Suzanne Lewis,
cruciform churches began to appear in the East to signify the conquest of Arianism—churches like that of Saint Babylas in Antioch.[37]
Lewis maintains that Ambrose dedicated his basilica, begun in 382,
to the cross of triumph after he finally maneuvered Gratian into
condemning the Arians at the Council of Aquileia (381). We shall
see that Ambrose made a point of dipping the cross into the baptismal waters in 386, where he called it the cross of triumph. This anti-
Arian Basilica Apostolorum may have helped provoke Valentinian's

Figure 1.6. Exterior of Basilica Virginum. Courtesy N. Wills.

court into attempting the seizure of the Basilica Portiana—and even the Basilica Nova—away from the triumphalistic Ambrose.

NORTH: THE BASILICA VIRGINUM (SAN SIMPLICIANO)

Ambrose repeated the cruciform plan of his Apostolorum in the single-naved church now known as San Simpliciano, renamed after the death of Ambrose for his successor as bishop, Simplician, the man who may have baptized Ambrose and who certainly counseled Augustine during his stay in Milan. This preserves more of the fourth-century structure than any of Ambrose's other churches. "The original structure survives nearly untouched."[38] The high walls with large window arches are still visible, having been bricked in (fig. 1.6). This, as a simpler pattern for cruciform churches, was immensely influential in the development of this type throughout northern Italy, becoming "the fountainhead of a large family of churches (fig. 1.7)."[39]

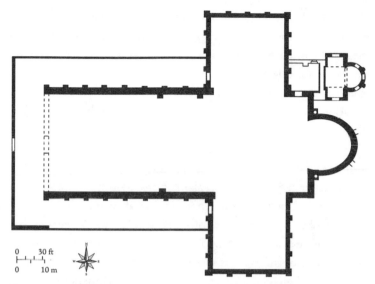

Figure 1.7 Plan of Basilican Virginum. From Richard Krautheimer, *Three Christian Capitals: Topography and Politics* (University of California Press, 1983), p. 68.

NORTHEAST: THE BASILICA PROPHETARUM (SAN DIONIGI)

The church later named San Dionigi, for Dionysius, an early bishop of Milan, was partly destroyed in the sixteenth century for a widening of the city walls, and entirely demolished in the eighteenth century, so there is no solid evidence of its plan. The name—Basilica of the Prophets—reflects Ambrose's own interest in the saints of the Old Testament (this will be discussed in chapter 6). The names of the churches ringing the city, though not given by Ambrose, certainly reflect his program for teaching and preaching—they are dedicated to prophets, apostles, martyrs, and virgins.

At the center of Ambrose's ecclesiastical imperium was the double cathedral he inherited when he was consecrated bishop. This was in the common form of two adjacent cathedrals. Some have thought the churches had different functions—one, say, as the bishop's seat, the other as a parish church; or one for special feasts, the other for the ordinary liturgy; or one as a martyrium, the other for celebrations of nonmartyrs. But Attilio Pracchi says that there is no evidence of different functions, only for seasonal rotation, with the Basilica Vetus as the main church from October to Easter and the Basilica Nova as the main church from Easter to October.[40] One did not rank above the other, or differ in dignity from its "twin." Though the evidence for these seasonal uses comes from a later time, it is not explained on any other grounds than antiquity, so Pracchi defends that usage as ancient.

Double cathedrals were often built side by side, but the Basilica Nova was added behind and slightly to the left of the Basilica Vetus. Perhaps this was because unevenness of the ground made it difficult to align them perfectly. In any event, the orientation of the altars toward the east was preserved. The Basilica Vetus is now under the huge gothic Duomo begun in the fourteenth century and completed in the nineteenth. Its separate baptistry is under the Duomo's sacristy, visited now beside the elevator taking people to the roof. The separate baptistries might have been used in Ambrose's time for women (the Vetus) and for men (the Nova).[41]

Though Ambrose established this complex ecclesiastical establishment, he did not do so without resistance and obstruction. It took all of his political savvy and ruthless determination to prevail over religious and imperial opponents and bring his ambitious plans to completion.

2

———

AMBROSIAN DISCIPLINE

W e do not know what Ambrose looked like. But we do know how he carried himself. As the secular governor of a province, he had been part of the Roman governing class, with its severe discipline for public figures, requiring a lofty posture, manly stride, resonant voice, and dignified gestures—all those things that ancient rhetoricians called *actio*.[1] The orator, said Cicero, should not have the trivial gestures of an actor but the weighty moves of an athlete (*De Oratore* 3.59). He should "express himself through his whole body, with a manly torsion from the waist" (*De Oratore* 18.59). The elder Seneca told his sons how to spot a future star orator: "Which of your peers has what I might call talent enough, or effort enough—but, more important, manliness enough" (*Controversiae* 1, Preface 9). Plutarch put public speaking among his "tips on health," since it makes for strength—"not a wrestler's strength, which builds layers of muscle like a structure's outer wall, but a strength that pervades with living energy one's vital and reacting limbs" (*Moralia* 130 AB).

Late antique Romans have been criticized for their politics of the person, not of policy or party. Modern historians have found the "overemphasis on moralizing and character" a peculiarly unsatisfactory feature of the historians of the age, such as Ammianus Marcellinus and Eunapius of Sardis.[2] But Peter Brown finds benefits embedded in the self-command required of this system:

> The huge ceremoniousness of late Roman life proved a two-edged weapon in the hands of those who wielded power. Ceremonious behavior was not only imposed from the imperial court down, but it also depended for its effectiveness on appealing to precisely the ideals of harmony and self-control associated with *paideia*. As a result, ceremony did not simply exalt the powerful; it controlled them, by ritualizing their responses and by bridling their raw nature through measured gestures. By so doing, ceremony insensibly worked the ideals of *paideia* into the texture of government. Only power wielded in a self-controlled and dignified manner carried full authority. Like neglect of procedure in a modern law case, neglect of the decorum silently and insistently imposed upon governors by the ceremonial that upheld their authority might at any moment invalidate their actions. *Aschémoneis hégemôn*, "Governor, you forget yourself": the phrase (placed in the mouth of a Christian martyr) was a rebuke that touched on the "symbolic Achilles' heel" of the powerful.[3]

Brown goes on, in a later passage, to show how the power of enacted *paideia* was of use to Ambrose in his conflict with the emperor Theodosius.[4] Not only had Ambrose internalized the whole mystique of self-command; he wrote three volumes of Stoic advice to inculcate these values in the clergy under him—his *De Officiis* (*Proper Conduct*).⁵ This was important not only for his own large body of priests and deacons but for the network of sympathetic bishops he enlisted to inculcate a similar discipline in other places (*O* 79). He wanted his churchmen to compete with the Roman senatorial class in terms of *gravitas* and *auctoritas*. His success in this endeavor is recognized by the Yale historian John F. Matthews: "Combining the talents of intellectual and rhetorician with those of diplomat and demagogue, Ambrose was the complete politician; and he stood at the center of a Christian court society of impressive style and accomplishment."⁶ It is worth quoting at some length what he required of his clergy to maintain this weighty enterprise. The passage displays Ambrose's striking satirical talent, as he drives home his points with sardonic zest.

> The set of a man's mind can be read in how he carries his body. This is how we size up "the hider in our heart"— ranking a man as frivolous, pretentious, and overwrought; or ranking him as weighty, determined, humble, and restrained. The mind speaks through the body's motions.
>
> Remember, sons, our associate who seemed to work hard at his assignments but whom I did not admit into our number for one reason only—that his body's carriage was unseemly. Or the other man, already in our number when I came here, whom I would not let walk ahead of me in procession since I winced as if whipped at the sight of his vain strutting—I maintained this even when, after his affronts, he came back for a while into our ranks. This was my only objection to these men, and my judgment was confirmed, since both fell from the faith, and what their gait revealed was confirmed in the unsteadiness of their commitment. One of them left behind true belief during

the Arian subversion, and the other, out of greed for money, pretended he was not a clergyman to evade trial before a bishop. Their mincing walk revealed their flighty character—that of flaneurs [*scurrai percursantes*].

Some, on the other hand, can barely be said to move at all, as if in studious pantomime, or like figures on a float bobbing slowly by, who seem to be beating out time with each step they take. Yet neither do I think it dignified to scurry around unless to cope with some real threat or necessary errand. Too often we behold people out of breath, their features twisted. Unless they are forced to hurry, this ugliness offends. I am not referring to those with rare but good reasons for haste but to those who have a way of being always in a bustle. So, in a word, I want neither one who moves like a robot [*simulacrum*] nor one who is running about in circles.

There is, after all, a proper pace, which conveys authority, serious consideration, and outward serenity—so long as straining for these does not betray itself in affectation. Transparent and simple action is called for, not displeasing pretense. Keep your motion natural—but if a defect is natural to you, concentrate on correcting it. Avoid posturing, but not improvement. (*O* 71–75)

As Ivor Davidson says of this passage: "Ambrose evidently had no shortage of applicants, if he could refuse a man simply because of his gait" (*O* 510).[7]

The gravitas Ambrose tried to instill in his clergy was something he had to work at acquiring himself. He was born to rule, but not by natural right. The son of a Praetorian prefect of Gaul, he became consularis (governor) at the age of thirty-three. Still, he was not what Romans would have considered truly highborn.[8] He belonged to the group Peter Brown calls "urban notables," a pool from which the Empire drew legal and administrative talent.[9] Even though Ambrose was not strictly of the senatorial class, Brown nonetheless strikes the right note about him when he writes: "Although he came from a senatorial family, Ambrose was not simply a Roman grandee. He belonged to the more insecure and interesting class of young nobles who sought imperial service because they needed power, and relished it."[10]

He was born (probably in 339) in the northern imperial capital of Trier, where his father held office under the emperor Constantine II. In 340 both Constantine and his father lost their lives, and Ambrose's mother took her three children to Rome, where she had important connections with the Christian community, including Pope Liberius, who presided over the formal ceremony in which her oldest child, Marcellina, took the veil of a consecrated virgin (*V* 3.1). These consecrated virgins were an important part of the church, especially in Rome (where Jerome had great influence with them). Famous benefactors of the Christian community, the virgins lived in an inner *cubiculum* of their family home.[11] So Ambrose grew up with his mother; his sister, Marcellina; and his older brother, Satyrus, in a very pious and well-connected family. Both sons were trained in the liberal arts, with a strong legal emphasis, and both entered the imperial service under one of the most powerful patrons of the time, Sextus Claudius Petronius Probus.

Probus, according to Alan Cameron, "had all the honors, power, and wealth a private citizen of that age could expect to win" (*LP* 775). He is described by Brown as "a notoriously power-hungry nobleman" and by John Matthews as "a spectacular profiteer."[12] Jerome said that his greed devoured provinces (*LP* 223). A member by marriage of the historically powerful Anician family, Probus was the son of a consul, a consul himself, the holder of four praetorian prefectures, and the grandfather of two briefly reigning emperors (Petronius Maximus and Olybrius). A Christian with an immense mansion in Rome, he would be buried next to St. Peter himself.[13] His wife, Anicia Proba, was a great patron of Rome's consecrated virgins. The poet Claudian says that Probus showered wealth on his numerous dependents.[14] Ammianus Marcellinus described him as "famous for his illustrious family, his influence, and his vast holdings," one who "raised his favorites to high office."[15] It was natural that Ambrose's mother, with a consecrated virgin as a daughter and two ambitious sons in Probus's Rome, would fall within the sweep of his benefactions. Ambrose caught his attention as a rising young legal advocate (P 5) and won office as an assessor to Probus while the latter was Praetorian prefect of Italy.

Through Probus's influence with Emperor Valentinian I, Ambrose became a consularis, with Milan in his jurisdiction. Valentinian, though he fiercely persecuted magic and witchcraft, tolerated most Christian and pagan cults.[16] Ambrose would obviously follow his imperial leader in this regard, so it is not surprising that, as the secular governor of Milan, he should be called on to adjudicate a conflict over the succession to Bishop Auxentius in that city. Auxentius had presided over the city for twenty years as an Arian. A pro-Nicene faction was trying to break this historic hold of the Arians on their city.

According to the long-accepted version of Ambrose's life, he proved so fair and just in handling this dispute that there was a unanimous outcry to make *him* the bishop. As if by divine prompting, a child first raised the cry, "Ambrose! Bishop!"

Ambrose tried to avoid the honor. He thought he could use his secular office to torture a person on trial, thus disqualifying himself for a sacred post. He declared his intention of retiring from the governorship to study philosophy. He invited prostitutes to his residence. He tried to flee the city. None of this worked. The people brought him back from flight and detained him while they petitioned the emperor in Trier to back their demand. All these details we get from Ambrose's first biographer, Paulinus, a man who knew him well since he had served as his secretary (P 6). Paulinus wrote his biography twenty-five years after Ambrose's death. He was asked to write it by Augustine, who was at the time (422 CE) making heavy use of Ambrose in his controversy with the Pelagians. Thus, as we might expect, the book is hagiographical. It shows Ambrose having visions (P 14, 29), healing illnesses (10, 44, 52), fighting demons (14–16, 21, 33, 48), and raising the dead (28). In Paulinus's work, opponents of Ambrose have an unhappy tendency to drop dead after crossing him (11, 18, 43, 54).

Despite all these obstacles to credibility, Paulinus for centuries continued to set the main lines of Ambrose's life story. He is the only intimate who recorded what went on during his episcopacy. He had access to materials now lost. Later biographers, who tried to eliminate or downplay the miraculous parts of the story, still relied on the book. Until quite recently, the most widely read biographical accounts—by (for instance) Frederick Homes Dudden, Jean-Rémy Palanque, or Angelo Paredi—followed the outline of Paulinus's narrative.[17] They agreed with him that Ambrose was made bishop by popular acclamation, that he quickly established his tests of orthodoxy, that he triumphantly overcame Arian challenges, and that he won over emperors with ease.

But there has been a modern revisionist movement in the study of Ambrose, skeptical of the claims that congealed around Paulinus's version. It is based on new material (like the opposition records from the Council of Aquileia), further study of "Arian" varieties (in the vein of Richard Hanson), archeological finds (at Santa Tecla and San Lorenzo), secular historians (like Ammianus Marcellinus), intense work on late antiquity (inspired by Peter Brown), and socioeconomic studies (following on those of A. H. M. Jones). On such bases, a new generation of historians has turned the old story upside down.[18]

The revisions start with Ambrose's election as bishop. Paulinus would have us believe that Ambrose was chosen by all because he was so universally respected, and that the Milanese instantly adopted Ambrose's Nicene views of the Trinity. In fact, the newly installed Ambrose was so sure of his home base that he could leave it almost immediately for a thousand-mile round-trip to the imperial seat at Sirmium, to oversee the installation of a Nicene bishop (P 11). This kind of interference in another see was noncanonical, but Paulinus wants to have Ambrose there to provoke the empress mother Justina, living at Sirmium, by inflicting a setback on her favored Arian cause. That is how Paulinus explains the origin of her vendetta against Ambrose when she moved with her son to Milan. Though the story of Ambrose's early victory so far from home was accepted by almost all the earlier Ambrose scholars (and even by some revisionists, like Neil McLynn and Roger Gryson), there is no basis for the story except Paulinus's word. Daniel Williams and others deny that it can have happened when and how Paulinus depicts.[19]

The revisionists argue that Ambrose would have had some difficulty taking over a see so firmly established as an Arian redoubt under four emperors (Constantius II, Julian, Jovian, Valentinian I). Auxentius did have some critics, both in Milan (e.g., Filastrius, future bishop of Brixia) and from outside the city (e.g., Hilary of Poitiers), but he survived them all for twenty years until his death.[20] His support cannot have evaporated overnight when Ambrose was elected. Ambrose may have tried at first to avoid being seen as the leader of Auxentius's adversaries—indeed, that could explain his theatrical attempts to resist the office of bishop. But the fact that sympathy for Auxentius continued to exist for some time is clear. When another Auxentius came to Milan, the Arian favorite of Justina, Ambrose said that his first name was actually Mercurinus but that he adopted the name of Auxentius "to mislead the flock that Bishop Auxentius had held" (*Epistulae* 75a.22). Why assume a borrowed popularity if that popularity did not exist?

Further, when the Goths took Roman prisoners at the battle of Adrianople (378), and Ambrose melted church plate to redeem the prisoners, his opponents were angered at this insult to Bishop Auxentius—since the plate had been donated to him by his Arian followers (O 136). Peter Brown writes, "By melting down the church plate of Milan in order to ransom prisoners of war in the distant Balkans, Ambrose of Milan, in fact, destroyed the memory of those Christian families (supporters of his Arian predecessor) whose names would certainly have been engraved on the edges of the great silver patens and along the rim of the Eucharistic chalices."[21] There was also resentment that Ambrose used some of the money from the melted Arian artifacts to build his new anti-Arian churches (O 142).

Ambrose says that his treatise on the Trinity, *De Fide*—his first theological treatise and only his second book (after a panegyric on virginity)—was commissioned in 378 by the emperor Gratian. That used to be taken as a sign that Gratian wanted instruction from Ambrose. Revisionists more plausibly think that the emperor, residing in a circle of Arians at Sirmium, was testing the new bishop on his views. When critics raised objections to *De Fide*, Ambrose had to follow up his book with a deeper treatment on the Holy Spirit. Ambrose, trained in legal and literary studies, had not undergone a thorough theological education. He had to bone up on doctrinal matters when rushed into the episcopacy. Even later on, Augustine would note how intently he pored over volumes in every bit of his spare time (C 6.3)

But revisionists are overstating their case when they mock this first exercise in theology. They rely on Arian notes in the margin of a *De Fide* manuscript.[22] Richard Hanson, for instance, writes of *De Fide*:

> Ambrose has not, like Athanasius and Hilary and Marius Victorinus, struggled with the problem of Arianism and thought it through for himself, but rather has learned the

conventional arguments because these are the stuff which the official, successful church hands out. Almost all his ratiocination proceeds upon the method (which is, admittedly, a weapon not unknown in Athanasius' armory) of assuming as true what he is supposed to be proving, and too often his arguments are, as rational discussion, beneath contempt.[23]

Ambrose was not ignorant but shrewd in his first tactical moves. He may have been a beginning theologian but he was a practiced lawyer. He states his position modestly (*De Fide* 1.4): "My preference is to encourage belief [*cohortare ad fidem*], not to define belief [*disputare de fide*]." The revisionists think Ambrose was blundering when he lumped together all non-Nicene views as "Arian." They prefer to call the opponents of Nicaea simply "anti-Nicene" or "homoian." But Ambrose was less ignorant than tactical. The Nicene view was that Jesus is, in relation to the Father, *homousios* (fully God), and the anti-Nicene view was that he is *homoiousios* (like God). There were many ways to define his likeness to God. Ambrose reduced them all to the basic formula: *Like* God is *not* God. To debate degrees of similarity was a distraction for him. Jesus either *is* God or he *isn't*. Revisionists complain that this was a trap. Exactly! Hanson thinks that Ambrose cheats when he calls the Arian Jesus unlike God (*dissimilis*) when they used the term *similis*. But for Ambrose, being merely *similis*, when the stakes are divinity itself, IS *dissimilis*.

The revisionists also take the side of the two Illyrians condemned at the Council of Aquileia (381)—Palladius, bishop of Riatiaria, and Secundinus, bishop of Singidunum. Gratian had called the council, meaning for it to be an ecumenical council of the whole Empire. But the Eastern emperor, Theodosius, simultaneously called his own council at Constantinople, which followed a firmly Nicene creed. The two condemned men at Aquileia complained that the meeting at Aquileia of a mere thirty-two Western bishops was unrepresentative. But it is hard to imagine their position improving if the stoutly anti-Arian bishops from Constantinople—or, for that matter, from Rome or Spain—had been added.[24]

Palladius claimed that Ambrose rigged the council, supplanting the nominal convener (the bishop of Aquileia), posting scribes behind the anti-Nicenes to spy on them, arranging the order of events so a letter of Arius was read and they were asked to agree or disagree with it, reducing them to quibbling over terms—or, in the case of Palladius, to pleading that he could not comment on Arius since he had never met him.[25] Ambrose, the Illyrians argue, rode roughshod over their minority position—which was true enough. But they were not above playing dirty themselves, as when they claimed that Ambrose had led a sexually promiscuous life before being invalidly consecrated bishop.[26] With Gratian's endorsement of the Council condemning all "Arians," Ambrose had a solid victory, which he celebrated in the "sign of the victorious cross" in his new Basilica Apostolorum. But Ambrose had a harder fight ahead of him, when the boy emperor Valentinian II and his Arian mother, Justina, came to Milan.

AMBROSE FIGHTS FOR HIS CHURCHES

Palaces belong to Emperors, churches to the bishop
—*Epistulae* 76.19

At first Ambrose moved diplomatically when Valentinian came to town, and scored some points with him in 383 and 384 (when the emperor was twelve and thirteen years old). When Gratian died in 383, the man suspected of his murder, Magnus Maximus, was a challenger for the role of Western ruler. Valentinian sent Ambrose to Trier to negotiate a truce with Maximus. The bishop was a logical choice for this role, since Maximus was (like Ambrose) pro-Nicene in his theology. But why would Ambrose accept the mission, since Valentinian had prominent *anti*-Nicene figures around him in his court? Presumably Ambrose thought he could deal with the power close to home more easily than his city could weather a war with Maxentius. Besides, Theodosius in the East was backing Valentinian, and Theodosius was decidedly Nicene. Ambrose must have thought support for Valentinian was the way to stick with the more powerful (and more orthodox) emperor of the East. In any event, he was successful in stalling Maximus and preventing war before Valentinian was prepared for it (see *Epistulae* 30).

Then, in 384, Ambrose supported Pope Damasus's effort in Rome to prevent the restoration of the pagan altar of Victory at the entrance to the Senate. Valentinian's advisers refused even to receive the delegation from the Senate. But by succeeding in this blocking action, Ambrose may have overplayed his hand. He told the emperor that the question of the altar was a religious issue, and if any imperial response was called for, it should issue from Theodosius, who had been given an emergency baptism during a dangerous illness, not from the unbaptized Valentinian. If, nonetheless, Valentinian should grant the pagans' request, then, Ambrose wrote, "We bishops could not take this lying down or ignore it. You may indeed come to church [after that], but you will not find a bishop there, or will find one opposing you" (*Epistulae* 72.13). If Ambrose was going to use control of his churches against the emperor, the court must have decided, then his churches should be taken from him. For the next two years that would be the obsessive aim of Valentinian's court, and of the queen mother, Justina. The campaign had four phases.[1]

PHASE ONE: COMMANDEERING THE BASILICA PORTIANA (EASTER 385)

The most important feast of the fourth-century church was that of Easter, with the solemn ceremonies of Holy Week and the important initiation of the newly baptized. This was one of those rare occasions when an emperor was expected to attend church services. Valentinian would be reluctant to attend Ambrose's church, the Basilica Nova, implicitly submitting to his authority, especially after Ambrose had threatened him precisely through control of the church.[2] The alternative would be to attend a different church, under a different bishop (Auxentius of Durostorum). This alternative service would even make possible the baptizing of Arian Christians in the yearly initiation rite. That is why the emperor's challenge took place just before Palm Sunday, the beginning of Holy Week and the day when the symbol (creed) was entrusted to the applicants for baptism.

This explains Ambrose's letter 75a, which records how the emperor tried to take over the Basilica Portiana outside the Porta Ticenese (the *porta* that gave the Portiana its name). As we saw earlier, this basilica was built as an imperial church, under Arian auspices. It could claim to be outside Ambrose's jurisdiction. Ambrose was summoned to the palace, to hear the demand that the Portiana be handed over. But Ambrose did not recognize an Arian claim to any of his churches. They were all under his orthodox jurisdiction. He appealed to the line of bishops who had held the see before Auxentius, quoting the words of Naboth, who refused to hand over his vineyard when Ahab was prodded into demanding it by Jezebel: "Never would I surrender my patrimony" (1 Kings 21.3): "So I too said: Never would I surrender the patrimony bequeathed to me by Dionysius (who died in exile defending the faith), bequeathed to him by the confessor-saint Eustorgius, bequeathed to him by Mirocles, and bequeathed to him by all the orthodox bishops who preceded him" (*Epistulae* 75a.18). This defense of his turf makes it clear that Ambrose—born in Trier, trained in Rome, entering imperial service at Sirmium—was now entirely in Milan, of Milan, Milanese to the bone.

Ambrose went to the palace when summoned, and Auxentius took this as a sign of timidity or surrender (*Epistulae* 75a.29). He said that Ambrose lacked "episcopal resolution" (*constantia sacerdotis*)—the last thing that could be said of Ambrose. But Ambrose had let his congregation know that he was going to turn down the demand for the Basilica Portiana, and his followers had marched on the church, meaning to occupy it:

When the people heard that I was going to the palace, they poured forth in a powerful rush that could not be checked as they offered themselves—against the imperial guard trying to scatter them—to die for their belief in Christ. Was I not begged then to quiet the crowd by prolonged persuasion, to extract from them a pledge that there would be no incursion into a religious basilica? And though it was my help that protected the guard, the fact that the people had rushed the church was held against me. (*Epistulae* 75a.29)

This first clash in the streets made clear to both Ambrose and his foes what his ace card was in this struggle with the emperor and his mother. It was the people of Milan, an instrument responsive to Ambrose's direction. What is often thought of as a contest between church and state was at ground level a standoff between Ambrose's congregation and the imperial guard, between people and army. Ambrose was headlong and unhesitating in his use of the people, while the army had to be cautious in its dealings with the garrison town—as it showed when it had to ask Ambrose to quiet his forces with "prolonged persuasion" (*multo sermone*). The emperor had the force of arms, but Ambrose had an effective neutralizer of that force.

PHASE TWO: THE ATTEMPT TO EXPEL AMBROSE FROM MILAN

As Ambrose says, the people's clash with the imperial guard was held against him. He was called a troublemaker and ordered to defuse the explosive situation by withdrawing from the scene. Paulinus even says that there were attempts to kidnap him and smuggle him out of town (P 12). Ambrose himself says that he was ordered out of town, and a wagon was kept ready for his removal (*Epistulae* 75a.1, 15). There was nothing new about expelling a bishop; that is how Constantius had got rid of Bishop Dionysius, to introduce Auxentius in

355. And the bishops condemned at Aquileia had already been ousted from Illyrium by Theodosius. But trying Ambrose for heresy would have been as ineffectual as Hilary's attempts to proceed against Auxentius had been. It was thought more effective to call Ambrose to account as a disturber of the peace. He was also charged with misuse of church money. "They hold it against me that I collect gold. (But I spend it on the poor.) They say that I recruit the poor with alms. I do have them as my defenders, but they defend me with their prayers" (*Epistulae* 75a.33).

The pressure and threats grew more intense as the winter came on. Believers were harassed as they went into or came out of Ambrose's services in his various churches. Late in the year Ambrose preached with soldiers all around the church he was in, and he praised those present for their courage in coming under such intimidation. He said they should not stay just to protect him—though that was clearly their intent (75a.4). He did not say what church he was in at the time. It could have been the Basilica Vetus, his winter cathedral. In 385 it could even have been his newly (or nearly) completed Basilica Martyrum, or the martyrium where he had buried his brother in 376—he notes that he went every day in 385 right past the palace on his way "to the martyrs' tombs" (*Epistulae* 75a.15). But it seems more likely he was in the contested Basilica Portiana, which he had refused to surrender and continued to treat as his. Here he kept up the defiant singing he had used to build morale against the foe (75a.34). This could have been seen as provocative to the court, which kept trying to tamp down Ambrose's "disturbance of the peace."

PHASE THREE: PRO-ARIAN LEGISLATION

On January 23, 386, the Emperor passed a law meant to prove that Ambrose was "contumacious" and treasonous toward authority (*Epistulae* 7 5.11). Codex Theodosianus 16.1.4 declares that anyone trying to prevent freedom of assembly for Arians commits treason and is subject to the death penalty.[3] Following this law, the emperor ordered Ambrose to the palace to debate his continued opposition to the Arians. In a taunt, Ambrose says that the willingness to discuss the law shows the court had doubts about its enforcement (*Epistulae* 75.9–11). In any case, Ambrose had no intention of obeying the summons. Religion should be discussed in church with believers, not in a palace, to be judged by laymen (*Epistulae* 75.17). If this was courting martyrdom, then so be it. Ambrose could call the emperor's bluff, sure that the people would not respond to his capture, imprisonment, or martyrdom with submission.

PHASE FOUR: OCCUPATION OF THE BASILICA NOVA

What could provoke Ambrose into an indefensibly flagrant violation of the January 23 law? If the Arians occupied the Basilica Nova, at the very time when Ambrose was about to move there for the Easter ceremony, and if Ambrose's people tried to oust them, that would be a clear violation of the law against interfering with an Arian service. As such, on the Friday before Palm Sunday, high officials from the court came to Ambrose with a demand that he hand over the Basilica Nova as well as the Portiana for Easter services by the Arian clergy (*Epistulae* 76.1–2). Ambrose said he could not surrender church properties. On the Saturday before Palm Sunday, the praetorian prefect came to say that the Portiana must be surrendered, if not the Basilica Nova. Ambrose again refused.

At the Palm Sunday mass, allies of Ambrose rushed to him with the news that the Basilica Portiana was being furnished with the accoutrements for imperial church attendance. (Special seating arrangements—for an emperor, along with his retinue and bodyguards—were necessary, properly furnished with purple hangings and other imperial insignia.)[4] Parts of his congregation went to occupy the Portiana, keeping the emperor's forces out.

Meanwhile, it was Ambrose's duty, after the Palm Sunday sermon, to instruct the competentes in the creed (the *traditio Symboli*). Normally, this would have taken place in a special catechumeneum, since the baptistry itself was not opened, revealing its interior, until dawn at Easter (G 5). On this day, since Ambrose feared that the Arians might try to prepare their own applicants in Holy Week at the Basilica Nova's baptistry, he moved his own competentes there for the Palm Sunday instruction. He writes his sister, "I began to perform the *traditio* in the basilica of the baptistry" (*in baptisterii basilica*), an unusual term for an unusual action (*Epistulae* 76.4).

The imperial guard, rather than trying to oust Ambrose's people from the Portiana, sealed it off with a cordon of men. Then Valentian imposed a curfew on the city, to keep "seditious" crowds off the streets (76.7). An Arian priest had been seized by Ambrosian sympathizers, and the bishop had to send emissaries to arrange for his release (76.5). Leading businessmen (*mercatores*) who supported Ambrose were accused of complicity with the crowds. Fines were imposed on them, and they were imprisoned when they could not instantly pay up. "Thus in the sacred days of Holy Week, when debtors are customarily released from prison, there was a clatter of chains hung around the necks of innocent men" (76.6).

In this war of nerves, with a standoff at the Portiana and the Basilica Nova under threat, the authorities were trying to drive a wedge between Ambrose and his principal weapon, the townspeople. Then the court played its trump card. Leaving the Portiana occupied, on Wednesday it sent soldiers into the Basilica Nova. It was commonly thought in the past that this was a military reclamation of the Portiana. But J. H. W. G. Liebeschuetz makes a persuasive case that it was the Basilica Nova that was taken. For one thing, Ambrose saw as he came out of his episcopal residence the soldiers entering the basilica (76.11). His home was near his cathedral, and he could not have seen from its doorway all the way to the Portiana, across town and outside the walls of the city. The court had leapfrogged the earlier ground of contention and carried the challenge directly into what was, in effect, Ambrose's front yard in the center of town.

Ambrose seemed to be caught in a perfect trap. He was called on to pacify his people. If he urged them to enter the Basilica Nova he would flagrantly be breaking the law against disrupting Arian services. He continued to pray all day with his people in the Basilica Vetus, keeping up their spirits with song. The congregation knew that Ambrose was threatened with imminent arrest, and they did not want to leave him exposed to danger. Augustine wrote of these tension-filled days: "The community piously kept vigil in the church, ready to die with their bishop your servant; and my mother, who attended on you, was with the foremost in supporting him and keeping watch, her whole life turned over to prayer" (C 9.15).

The loud devotions being carried on just outside the Basilica Nova drew some curious soldiers over to the twin church next door. Their entry frightened the community, but the soldiers protested that they were just there to join in the prayers (76.113). Some people in the Vetus called on Ambrose to lead them in procession to "the other basilica"—another indication that the Nova was meant, since a march through the city and outside the walls was hardly feasible. Ambrose knew that even trying to force an entry at the basilica next door would be foolhardy—and was just what the court was tempting him into doing. Protesting that he did not want to use the people as a shield, Ambrose left the basilica at night to go to his home. If the emperor's men wanted to seize him, he would give them this clear chance (86.11).

On Thursday, Ambrose preached a sermon on the sufferings of Job. "I rose up to admire a single Job, and found multiple Jobs to admire. In each of you I saw a Job redivivus, with the patience and strength of that singularly holy man glowing in you." He pictured each of them addressing the emperor this way: "We entreat you, Caesar—we do not fight you, but we do not fear you—we entreat you. This is proper for us as Christians, that the serenity of peace may be wished for, and the firmness of our belief in the truth shall not falter from any fear of death" (76.14).

On Good Friday, "the day when the Lord offered himself up for us, and when penitents in the church are forgiven," the emperor ordered his troops out of the basilica and returned all the fines exacted from the mercatores. Ambrose wrote to his sister, "What joy in the whole people, what applauding, what thanks!" (76.26). The emperor not only yielded, but left town to celebrate Easter elsewhere.[5] Ambrose had won the war of nerves, and done so without violent confrontation. Ivor Davidson aptly writes:

> By a skilful if impromptu combination of brinkmanship, demagoguery, and exploitation of popular emotions, he engineered a remarkable coup, resisting both the surrender of property and open debate with Auxentius. The *populus Dei*, locked inside its sanctuary, sang its hymns and prepared to face martyrdom in fidelity to its cause, while the forces of Satan—the imperial troops dispatched to forestall public disorder—prowled at its doors. (O 71)

Remember that in 383 Ambrose celebrated the victory with Gratian at the Council of Aquileia by building the "sign of the cross" Basilica Apostolorum. Now, in 386, he celebrated the victory over Valentinian by consecrating his new Basilica Martyrum with a spectacular discovery of new martyr relics. Finding the bodies of the martyrs was a kind of victory lap, a way of saying to Justina, "Can you top this?" As Augustine writes: "At this point you sent a vision to the bishop I have mentioned, revealing where the bodies of the martyred Gervase and Protase lay hidden. For years you had preserved them incorrupt in your secret treasury, and now was the right time to bring them forth, to check the ravings of a woman who was also a queen" (C 9.16). The victory of finding the relics was crowned with a series of acclaimed miracles worked by the saints.

Peter Brown can help us understand the importance of relics in late antiquity. He argues that they, even more than creeds and councils, wove together the Christian unity. They were an assurance of heaven's presence at many centers, and their transfer, the processions and pilgrimages prompted by them, the miracles worked by them, were a guarantee of orthodoxy. That is why the mere finding of the remains of Gervase and Protase was taken as a refutation of the Arian heresy and a pledge of Nicene belief.[6]

This hard-fought battle with Valentinian made it easier for Ambrose to win his conflicts with the emperor Theodosius when he succeeded to the Western Empire along with the Eastern—forcing him to withdraw his order that the bishop of Callinicum rebuild a synagogue destroyed by Christians in 388, and making him repent the massacre of rioters in Thessalonica in 390. But those victories followed after Augustine left Milan in 386. For this book, we must wonder what Augustine was doing in Milan while the town seethed with impending violence during Ambrose's fight for his churches. The somewhat surprising answer is that he was doing nothing.

AUGUSTINE ON THE WAY TO MILAN

The early life of Augustine is well known from *Confessions*—how he was born in the North African town of Tagaste in 354; acquired a common law wife as a teenager, with whom he had a son; became a Manichean in Carthage, where he first studied and then taught rhetoric; and left Africa for Rome in 383, when he was twenty-nine years old. In Rome he taught rhetoric. An oration he gave on a set topic brought him to the attention of the city's prefect, the famous senator Quintus Aurelius Symmachus, who had been asked by the court in Milan to recommend an imperial orator (C 5.23). This "Rome-Milan axis," as Neil McLynn calls it, was meant to keep relations cordial between the old center of the Western Empire and the new one: "The parvenu capital looked south to Rome for talent and to borrow the luster of its cultural credentials; [in Rome] the senatorial aristocracy in turn needed its outlets at the court of Milan."[1]

Yet relations between the two cities—and especially between Bishop Ambrose and Senator Symmachus—were somewhat strained during the time when Augustine was in Rome. Two years before Symmachus was appointed prefect of the city in 384, he had led a senate delegation to Milan, asking the emperor Gratian to restore an altar of the goddess Victory at the entrance to the Senate. The emperor Constantius II had removed the altar in 357, since it did not accord with the empire's now-Christian government. Another emperor (presumably Julian the Apostate) later restored it; but then Gratian removed it again, along with the subsidies to temples and the Vestal Virgins. Symmachus, speaking for the pagan senators still active in Rome, wanted the altar and the subsidies returned. Gratian's advisers refused even to grant Symmachus an audience. It used to be thought that Ambrose effected this rebuke, but the revisionists now doubt that (*LP* 35–37). There were at least six embassies to the court on this matter over the years, and the emperors had vacillated while trying to keep the peace between assertive Christians and fading pagans.[2]

In 383, the year Augustine arrived in Rome, the emperor Gratian was murdered and the boy-emperor Valentinian II succeeded him (the one for whom Ambrose performed the embassy to his rival Maximian). It seemed a good time to renew the effort for the altar's restoration. Symmachus did not risk another personal humiliation by going to the court himself. Instead he sent a *relatio* (official dispatch) using all his rhetorical ability to make the case for an old tradition (the altar had been raised by Augustus to celebrate the defeat of Antony and Cleopatra at Actium in 31 BCE). The bishop of Rome, Damasus, alerted the bishop of Milan, Ambrose, to this new challenge to official Christianity, and Ambrose fired off a letter to Valentinian before he had read the *relatio* (*Epistulae* 72). Valentinian's advisers again rejected the request to restore the altar. And Ambrose took the occasion to deliver a studied rejection of all Symmachus's claims for pagan tradition. Augustine was traveling to Milan as this letter was being absorbed by its audience, and he no doubt got his first impression of Ambrose, even before meeting him, from this scathing attack on his own patron, Symmachus.

The exchange between Ambrose and Symmachus has become famous, as, in the words of Alan Cameron, "a direct confrontation between the leading pagan and the leading Christian of the age" (*LP* 40). For a long time it has been placed in the context of a supposed pagan revival in the late fourth century. But Cameron has sifted an impressive body of evidence to show that there was no such revival (*LP* 355–420). Augustine, who was at both Rome and Milan during the fight over the altar and its aftermath, does not mention the altar. But as a professional rhetorician he must have sized up the performances of the two men who were so important to his life at the time. It surely influenced his cautious first assessments of Ambrose.

The argument over the altar has become famous, and deserves consideration. Symmachus made four basic points:

I. RELIGIOUS PLURALISM

Appealing to the imperial tradition of Valentinian I, who (despite his Christianity) tolerated religious differences, Symmachus said that suppressing variety of beliefs was a limitation on the ways of knowing a mysterious God.

> Everything is filled with god. . . . Since reason is entirely in the dark, what surer guide is there than acknowledgment of past omens taken from memory and history? . . . We ask only for peaceful treatment of the ancient gods, the local gods. It is reasonable that we all worship a single power. We all contemplate the same stars, we share one sky, we are surrounded by the same cosmos. What does it matter what each one's opinion of the truth is? There is no single path toward so great a mystery. Why quibble endlessly when it is prayer not disputation we are seeking? (5, 8, 10)[3]

2. SOCIAL COHESION

Ancient practice makes for continuity in the body politic.

> What better serves the glories of the past than the defense
> of what our ancestors instituted, the laws and the greatness
> of our fatherland, and what serves you better than a sense
> that you cannot tamper with the ancient ways? . . . Each
> one's ways, each one's rituals suit him. Divine intelligence
> has fit different religious practices to preserve every city,
> and protectors of their destiny are given to them as souls
> are given men at their birth. (2, 8)

The local patriotism for the cults and shrines, embedded in a long
history, were not easily uprooted, and Symmachus said that the
consequences of ignoring these ties would be dire. For instance,
senators swore oaths on the Victory altar at the beginning of each
session, and he said this pledged them against perjury—why risk
removing such a helpful inhibition (5)?

3. FIDELITY TO CONTRACT

The hereditary estates pledged by donors to shrines and to the care
of the Vestals should not be violated to fill imperial coffers.

> Honorable fundraising should not be tainted with this
> kind of income. The budget of honorable princes should be
> increased by plunder from enemies, not by exactions from
> priests. What profit comes from such dishonor? (12)

Symmachus argues that it is disgraceful not to keep the Vestal Virgins in their accustomed dignity and the priests of ancient rituals
in their contractually supported services. Animal sacrifices were
paid for by private bequests, and the rights of the donors should be
respected.

The history of Rome's victorious expansion was inextricably inter-
twined with religious devotion. Symmachus presented a moving
picture of the personified Rome addressing the Western and Eastern emperors Valentinian and Theodosius:

> You finest emperors, fathers of our fatherland, honor my
> old age, which religious rites have prolonged. Let me con-
> tinue living with the customary ceremonies, for which I
> have nothing to regret. Let me, born free, live on in my own
> way. This religion brought the whole world under my sway,
> and beat off Hannibal from my walls, and the Senones from
> my Capitol. Was I preserved then only to be cast off in my
> old age? Must I see some new arrangements thought proper
> now, when innovation comes too late and as an insult? (9)

Symmachus contrasts the long history of Roman victories with
recent droughts and famine brought on after animal sacrifice at the
Roman altars was suspended (15–16).

Ambrose answered this showpiece appeal for the old religious
ways with a long and careful response of his own. The two arguments are surprising. One would think the pagan would speak for
a rational world and the Christian for a mystical one. But Symmachus was appealing for sentiment and the past, so Ambrose would
appeal to practical and progressive forces, to the future. The pagan
gave us a personified Rome begging for mercy. The bishop shows
this figure as a hag fed up with bloody sacrifice and looking for
late-life change. Symmachus went for pathos, Ambrose for satire.
Here is his Rome speaking:

> What is it with this senseless daily shedding of innocent
> animals' blood? Victories are derived from the nerves of

warriors not the guts of cattle. That is not the toughness [*disciplina*] with which I conquered the world. Camillus by combat brought back the standards to the Capitol after slaying the Gauls who had seized the Tarpeian Rock. Courage regained what religion did not protect. No need to mention Attilius dying in battle. Africanus prevailed over the battle lines of Hannibal not on the altars of the Capitol. What is all this talk of ancient rites? I despise the rites of the Neros. What need to bring up emperors who lasted a day, or those who fell as soon as they rose? Do you think it is a new thing for barbarians to break in? What about those non-Christian emperors, one of whom was taken prisoner (the first time that happened), and the other whose world was imprisoned, while their sacrifices for victory earned them nothing. Who claims the altar of Victory had been removed in their time?

In my white-haired old age, I am ashamed of all that sacrificial blood, but I am not ashamed to have become a convert at last, at the same time as the world was converting. No age is too old to learn. The only thing to blush at is refusing to learn. White hairs should boast not of their years but of their wisdom. There is no shame in improving with age. I was like the barbarians when I did not know God. The old sacrifices were just a drenching in blood. Why look for heavenly pronouncements in dead cattle? Come learn of heavenly conquest on earth. Here we live, but there we conquer. Let God, who made me, teach me heaven's secrets, not some man who does not understand himself. Who more than God should I trust? Why do you believe when you do not know what you worship? (*Epistulae* 73.7)

Ambrose pitted against a timeless and retrospective Rome a kind of religious proto-Darwinian world itching to move on.

He says old rituals must be preserved. But everything has changed for the better. The universe itself began with a dark coagulation of elements in the blank horror of space. (23)

Symmachus praised animal sacrifice at the altars. Ambrose speaks of martyrs' deaths at the hands of tyrants.

> We take pride in such blood, while they are worrying about bequests. We treasure our sign of triumph while they are worried by what peeves them. They never did us a better favor than when they ordered that Christians should be beaten, forbidden, and executed. Our piety took as a prize what their perfidy imposed as punishment. (11)

Symmachus lines up his decorous Vestals as in a classical frieze. Ambrose answers with a parade of Christian virgins who live in perpetual chastity without any bequests to reward them:

> He says, "Let the Vestals have their bequest!" That is how people talk who think there cannot be an unfunded virginity. They rely on bribes rather than on purity. And how many virgins does their money buy them? A bare seven Vestals are installed. That is all they get with their sacred headbands, their purple-dyed robes, their pomp of floats through crowded streets, their political privilege, their lucrative salaries, and their limited tenure of abstinence!
>
> Let them turn their mind and eyes elsewhere—to a chaste race, a people of virtue, a polity of virgins. No ceremonial headbands here, just a humbly practical veil, regally chaste. No enhancements of beauty but renunciation of it. No gorgeous robes, no ornamental indulgences, but a discipline of fasting. No bequests, no payments. You might think they would tire of their regimen as they prolong it.

But it strengthens as they continue it. Chastity is its own reward. A virginity purchased and not embraced for itself is no true virginity. A purity auctioned for pay and for a time is not real. (11–12)

Symmachus must have felt like the various emperors Ambrose tackled. He thought he was engaging in a civilized debate, and he found himself instead up against a street fighter. Ambrose trumped Vestals with nuns, sacrificial cattle with bloody martyrs, and a weeping Rome with a worn-out woman repenting her ways.

Augustine's sympathies were probably with Symmachus in this war of words. He had spent his twenties lecturing on Vergil, a poet much admired by Symmachus, praising the Rome of Aeneas and his gods. Like any provincial, he must have been impressed, on his arrival in Rome, by the physical presence of a pagan past, the past he had tried to pass on to his students. For him the salon of Symmachus renewed the life of learned leisure Augustine admired in the dialogues of Cicero—a life he would recreate in the villa at Cassiciacum, his own first scholarly retreat (*LP* 396–98). Though this is only my guess, I think he preferred the dignified restraint of Symmachus's *relatio* to the tabloid style of Ambrose, with his butchered martyrs and sensational picture of Rome as a haggard woman. This helps explain his initial resistance to Ambrose. As we shall see in the next chapter, he thought Ambrose something of a bully and demagogue. Among other obstacles, Ambrose liked to show off his knowledge of Greek, which would always make the Greekless Augustine somewhat uncomfortable. Ambrose and Augustine were temperamentally very different. No wonder, then, that Augustine later thought only providence could explain their eventual interaction.

AUGUSTINE IN MILAN

By the time he wrote *Confessions*, twelve years after his baptism, Augustine treated his appointment to the court in Milan as a providential move by God, to bring him under the influence of Ambrose.

> And so I reached Milan and Ambrose, the bishop ranked among the best men in the world, your faithful servant, whose eloquence tirelessly provided your people with lavish food and gladdening oil and wine of sober intoxication. He assumed a father's role toward me, to guide my wanderings with a bishop's loving care. I responded at first with an affection based not on his preaching of the truth, which I was sure could not be found in your church, but on his kindness to me as a person.

Based on passages like that, it was for centuries assumed or asserted that Augustine was converted by Ambrose. Later in life, Augustine would find it useful to encourage that view. But it was not his view at the time of his stay in Milan.

In the *Soliloquia*, written in the months just before his baptism, in the millionaire's villa at Cassiciacum, he deplores the cruelty with which Ambrose refused to give him any guidance toward the faith. Reason, speaking to Augustine, says that Ambrose could instruct him on the true meaning of life, and Reason wonders why he did not ask for that instruction. But Augustine answers:

> The one thing I regret is that I was not able to reveal my interest in him or in his wisdom. In that case he would have pitied my thirst and quenched it before now. He is totally confident that he has the whole argument for the immortality of the soul, so he does not realize that others experience great suffering from their lack of knowing this, and that it is cruel [*crudele*] not to help them in their quest.[1]

It is clear from this that Augustine wanted to discuss his personal problems with Ambrose, but the great man had no time for it. At one point in *Confessions*, he asks himself where he can go to seek wisdom, and gives himself the disappointing answer, *"Non vacat Ambrosio"*—Ambrose is too busy (C 6.19). Ambrose remained a mystery to him, one whose face betrayed nothing about his interior. There is a touching scene where Augustine visits Ambrose, hoping to converse with him, and he is forced to sit with others as they watch their bishop intently studying his Greek texts.

> My impulse was for intellectual challenge. I itched for argument. As for Ambrose, I thought him a prosperous man, as the world judges, respected by the successful, though I counted his celibacy against him. I had no way of knowing about—I was totally excluded from—whatever aspirations he might entertain, what struggles against the temptations of his high place, what solace he found when he was

baffled. His face gave no clue to what went on in his heart, to any interior joy he might savor while feeding on you, his bread. He, on his side, was no more aware of my own seethings, of the pit that was opening before me.

I could not ask him the questions I wanted, in the way I wanted, since I was sealed off from his hearing and responses by a crowd of those who had business with him, and whose needs he catered to. When he was free (but only for a time) from these importunities, he restored his body with food and his mind with books. When he read his eyes scanned the page and his heart seized the meaning, while he formed no words with his lips. Often, when we were present—since he did not restrict access to himself, and the names of visitors were not announced—we watched him read, silently as he always did, and after we had been sitting there in a prolonged silence (with none so cheeky as to break his spell) we withdrew.

We supposed that he had so little time he could call his own, for restocking his mental store, beset as he was by the problems of others, that he resisted involvement in more such affairs. He might have avoided reading a passage out loud before an alert listener since he could be asked to explicate it, leading to discussion of nice points. Time squandered that way would cut back on the number of books he wanted to peruse. He might also have found that silent reading helped preserve his voice, which tended to grow hoarse.

Whatever his reason, he clearly acted wisely. But that meant, as well, that I had no opportunity to raise the points on which I wished to consult your holy oracle in his breast. I was limited to brief exchanges. Only if he were free for a long session could my seething be fully explained to him, and that session never came. (C 6.3–4)

The myth of Ambrose as the source of Augustine's conversion was saved for a while by the most influential study of Augustine in the mid-twentieth century, Pierre Courcelle's *Recherches sur les Confessions de Saint Augustin*. Courcelle claimed that, even though Augustine could not bare his soul to Ambrose in private sessions, he heard Neoplatonic doctrine on the immateriality of the soul in Ambrose's Sunday sermons, which he attended with his mother, and these were the key factor in his conversion to Nicene Christianity.[2] This book set off a scholarly scramble to find Neoplatonist features in the Ambrosian sermons Augustine might have heard. For a while this was the focus of research on Augustine's days in Milan. But the Ambrosian revisionists and modern Augustinians have punctured this scholarly fad.

An initial problem is that Courcelle says it was the Neoplatonism of Ambrose's Sunday sermons that proved the crucial factor in Augustine's conversion. Yet we do not know what Sunday sermons he heard (as opposed to the catechetical instruction he later received). It is true that Augustine says he went to hear Ambrose preach "every Day of the Lord [Sunday]" (C 6.4), but we need not take this very literally. He had many court duties to attend to, and a growing circle of intellectual friends who took up his time. He tells us he was absent from Ambrose's most spectacular Sundays of his second year in Milan—the showdown with Valentinian on Palm Sunday and Easter (C 6.15) and from the festivities around the installation of the Gervase and Protase relics (C 6.16).

He says he began attending Ambrose's sermons out of professional curiosity about his rhetorical technique. In some ways he found him inferior to his old Manichean friend-foe Faustus:

I brought a technical interest to his discourses with the congregation, not for the motive I should have had but to

see if he lived up to his reputation. Was he more or less el-
oquent than report had registered? Weighing carefully his
style, I treated the content with a lofty disregard. I ap-
proved his easy fluency, which was more learned than that
of Faustus, but—in style at least—less witty and charming.
(C 5.23)

But in time some of Ambrose's content began to register with him:

Though I did not care to learn what he was preaching, only
to hear how he was preaching it—this silly interest being
all I was capable of, since I had no expectation that he
could lead me to you—yet some of this content, which I
was not following, slipped into my thoughts along with the
style I was following closely. I could not keep them apart.
While I had an open mind for what he was saying deftly,
what he was saying soundly reached me also, though only
by degrees. (C 5.24)

At this point, sure enough, Augustine says he started learning
just the things Courcelle wants him to be learning from the Sunday
sermons—the existence of "pure spirit" (C 6.4) and the "symbolic" un-
derstanding of the Hebrew scriptures. But here, too, there are signs
that Augustine is retroactively "adopting" Ambrose as his spiritual
father. Take the second point first, the typological reading of the
Hebrew scripture as foretelling the gospels. Augustine did eventually
adopt that, as a result of the intense daily instruction he would get for
baptism in 387. But at the end of 386, when he asked Ambrose to
suggest appropriate reading before his baptism, Ambrose recom-
mended Isaiah—and Augustine could not make Ambrosian or allegorical or any other sense of the prophet, and had to set the book aside
(C 9.13). Why would he be at such a loss if he had already learned
Ambrose's method of reading the Old Testament, especially since he

later said of Isaiah that "more clearly than others he foretold the gospel and the calling of the gentiles" (C 9.13)?

As for Ambrose's revealing to him the possibility of "pure spirit," Augustine had other and better sources for that teaching—and sources he acknowledged and thanked at the time. The first of these was Mallius Theodore, a friend he idolized both for Neoplatonist learning and for what he took as his moral excellence. It was Theodore who introduced him to the "books of the Platonists" (C 7.13), translated into Latin so Augustine could read them. Augustine especially admired the fact that Theodore had given up a flourishing political career to live in quiet reflection as a Christian scholar (this would be Augustine's own goal just after his baptism). The court poet Claudian also praised Theodore for his retirement to Milan to study Neoplatonist philosophy. As he put it,

> Athens, dislodged, comes to your Latin home . . .
> Your Plato by his teaching raised his country.[3]

Besides philosophical and astronomical studies, Theodore wrote Latin philosophical dialogues—and Augustine would write the same kinds of dialogues in his retreat before his baptism. Claudian said of Theodore:

> Crabb'd Greek to Latin you transform,
> With skill at shaping urbane interchanges
> A tapestry of truth from crossing strands.[4]

Augustine expressed his great debt to Theodore by dedicating his prebaptism dialogue *De Beata Vita* to the man he felt had already reached that blessed state (he would later reject the idea that one can be happy anywhere short of heaven).[5]

Here is part of the effusive dedication to Theodore:

Since, my Theodore, I look only to you for what I need, impressed by your possession of it, consider what type of man is here present to you, what state I believe I am in, what kind of help I am sure you can give me.... I came to recognize, in the conversations about God held with our priest friend and you, that He is not to be considered as in any way corporeal.... After I read a few books of Plotinus of whom I realized you are a devotee, and tested them against the standard of the sacred writings, I was on fire....

So I beg you, by your own goodness, by your concern for others, by the linkage and interaction of our souls, to stretch out your hand to me—to love me and believe you are loved in return and held dear. If I beg this, I may, helped by my own poor effort, easily reach the happiness in this life that I suspect you have already gained.

That you may know what I am doing, how I am con-ducting my friends to shelter, and that you may see in this my very soul (for I have no other means to reveal it to you), I thought I should address you and should dedicate to your name this early discourse, which I consider more religious than my other ones and therefore worthy of you. Its subject is appropriate, since together we pondered the subject of happiness in this life, and I hoped no gift of God could be greater than that. I am not abashed by your eloquence (why should that abash me which, without rivaling it, I honor?) nor by the loftiness of your position—however great it is, you discountenance it, knowing that only what one masters can turn a truly favorable countenance on one.[6]

Claudian praises the way the younger Theodore sped up the rungs of the Roman cursus honorum (58–60), becoming praeto-rian prefect for Gaul in 382. Then he praises his retired life as a scholar in Milan (the time when Augustine became his friend and disciple). But Claudian says that the goddess Justice herself summoned him back to governmental service, where he took the Empire-wide office of consul in 399. What Claudian treats as the crown of a brilliant career Augustine considered a desertion, saying that Theodore, plunging back into the political vanities, became "inflated with raging winds of pride" (C 7.13). The man whose pious life of learning he had taken as a pattern for his own ambitions had betrayed that ideal. In his *Retractiones*, written late in life to list and assess all his writings, Augustine regretted his dedication of *De Beata Vita*:

> I regret that I attributed more than I ought to Mallius Theodore, to whom I dedicated this book, though he was a learned man and a Christian. (1.2)

It will be noticed that in his dedication Augustine wrote of "the conversations we held about God with our priest friend." Courcelle and others took this as a reference to Ambrose. But we have seen that Augustine denies ever having had an occasion for intimate conversation with Ambrose, and there is no evidence that Theodore was in any way close to Ambrose (if he had been, he could have made Augustine part of that company). No, Augustine is obviously referring to the priest who welcomed his company and led him toward the renunciations of the garden—Simplician. With Simplician he had the discussions that Ambrose had no time for. The fifth-century church historian Gennadius of Massilia explains why Augustine would have found Simplician's ways more inviting than those of Ambrose: "By asking questions like a student, he became the teacher of those he asked."[7]

James O'Donnell says of Simplician: "He was the true center of the 'Milan circle,' such as it was; he got his Platonism from the best Latin Platonist of the time, [Marius] Victorinus. The *De Philosophia* of Ambrose is likely to be close to what Simplician would have said himself." Simplician had been Ambrose's instructor in Greek philosophy. Ambrose addressed him this way:

> You have scoured all the earth for the sake of your beliefs and the acquisition of knowledge, and have spent your entire life in continual reading by day and by night, and by penetrating intellect have sifted all things knowable, so as to distinguish truth from falsehood in philosophy books, including those too empty for them to outlast their writers' lives.[8]

That last sentence chimes with what Augustine wrote about his first meeting with Simplician, that the priest was cheered to hear that Augustine had been reading "certain writings of the Platonists," since, he wrote, "I had not chanced on other Philosophers' writings, dense with sophistries and false leads inspired by worldly principles, but on writings haunted in all kinds of ways by God and his Word" (C 8.3)

Simplician was so respected in Milan that, on Ambrose's recommendation (P 46), he became its bishop when Ambrose died in 397, and on his death three years later he was canonized and the Basilica Virginum was renamed for him—Sancti Simpliciani. Augustine said that Simplician was Ambrose's "father in receiving grace," which means that Simplician baptized Ambrose when he was elected bishop. Paulinus wrote that Ambrose did not want to be baptized by the Arians who surrounded his predecessor in Milan (P 9), and Simplician was devoutly pro-Nicene.

Even after Simplician's death, Augustine recalled fondly his conversations with him in Milan, writing in *The City of God*: "According to the saintly old Simplician, whom I regularly consulted [*solebamus audire*] before he became the bishop of Milan, a certain Platonist was in the custom of saying that this opening [of the Gospel according to John] should be inscribed in gold letters and posted in the most prominent place of every church."⁹ And while Simplician was still alive, and he and Augustine were both bishops, the old mentor from Milan wrote Augustine to enquire about certain Bible passages (the student still proving a teacher). Augustine wrote a lengthy answer (*De Diversis Quaestionibus ad Simplicianum*), and wrote in his accompanying letter: "The heartfelt affection you show in your letter is not a new and untried vintage to me but a familiar and treasured taste brought up from the cellar" (*Epistulae* 37.1). Augustine never corresponded with Ambrose after he left Milan.

So Augustine had direct access to Neoplatonist thought in his frequent conversations with Mallius Theodore, Simplician, and their circle. He did not need to extract it piecemeal from Ambrose's Sunday sermons, as Courcelle thought. More to the point, he had taken from that thought the thing he most needed—a belief in pure spirit—long before he wanted to discuss his personal problems with Ambrose or Simplician. His so-called conversion in the garden was not a matter of intellectual difficulty. Those problems had been solved well before he decided to ask for baptism:

> I was sure, now, that you lived outside time, though I saw this "as in a mirror's wavering image." I no longer questioned the fact that there is one reality that cannot decay, from which are derived all other realities. Now I wanted more to rest in you than to reason about you. (C 8.1)

When he says that he wanted help from Ambrose for his "seethings," it was not a matter of intellect but of will that he was concerned about—his personal wrestling with the choice he felt compelled to make. For him, a full Christian life demanded a philosophical detachment from the body. From the time when, as a teenager, he read Cicero's *Hortensius*, he had felt that his body was an obstacle to the higher life of the mind. Cicero had said that it was like the corpses that pirates tied to their prisoners, face to face.[10] He felt he could not give himself entirely to God while he was still tied to sexual gratification. What he needed now was not intellectual persuasion but a strengthening of the will. He was not sidling up to a mental conversion but to a spiritual vocation. So most of the tales told him in this crucial moment were not of people changing their religion (the normal meaning of conversion) but of their embracing a hard choice in their mode of life—the friends of Pontician breaking off their marital engagements to embrace the monk's life (C 8.15–18), Anthony giving up all his wealth to the poor (C 8.29), Marius Victorinus risking his worldly career to accept baptism and then giving up his teaching post in Rome to study theology (C 8.3–5, 10).

This last story was told to Augustine by Simplician, who artfully pointed out the similarities to Augustine's own problem—both men were convinced of the Christian truth but were held back by attachment to worldly satisfactions. Victorinus was an orator in the service of Rome, for which he had been rewarded with a statue in the Forum of Trajan. "No sooner had I heard Simplician's tale of Victorinus than I was on fire to do as he did—and no wonder: that is why he had told it to me" (C 8.10). This is the kind of counsel and encouragement Augustine had hoped to get from Ambrose. It was Simplician who correctly diagnosed his problem and the best way to address it. Augustine felt he had been guided by God to seek out Simplician:

> You then prompted me—and I saw on consideration how wisely—to approach Simplician—he was your good servant, I could see, glowing with your bounty. Beyond that, I had learned at second hand how true to you he had been from his childhood, and I considered him now, after his living long and deeply mulling the way your path should be followed, to be a man great in experience and learning—as

he proved to be. I determined to consult him about my seethings that he might produce from his store a rule for one in my condition to tread your path. (C 8.1)

It is hard to understand, after reading of the effect on Augustine of Mallius Theodore and Simplician, how so many people continue to think that Ambrose converted Augustine or brought him to either Neoplatonism (the Courcelle thesis) or to the church (the hagiographical tradition). This is especially true when we consider what Augustine was doing in the year before his baptism. The two principal events in Ambrose's career during that time were his struggle with the emperor and his mother over possession of his churches and the finding of the remains of the martyrs Gervase and Protase. Augustine, by his own account, kept his distance from both tremendous developments. He was not inside Ambrose's church when it was under siege. His mother was there:

> The community piously kept vigil in the church, ready to die with their bishop your servant, and my mother, who attended on you, was with the foremost in supporting him and keeping watch, her whole life turned over to prayer. (C 9.15)

But he was not with her. "We were more cool on the matter, since your Spirit had not yet thawed us."

As for the finding of the martyrs, and the spectacular outburst of miracles around the relics, Augustine would, eleven years later in *Confessions*, profess a belief in that sequence. But what he wrote about miracles at the time was not only skeptical but dismissive. Between the discovery of the bodies and his baptism, writing from his villa retreat, he mocked those "daunted by hollow claims of the miraculous," and three years later he was still opposed to the demagoguery of promoting miracles: "Miracles have not been allowed to stretch into our time, or the soul would always be looking for sensations, and the human race would grow jaded with their continual occurrence."[11]

In fact, Augustine disapproved of Ambrose's whole bustling world of power and contention. His model was Mallius Theodore, who at that time had retired from politics and the active life, and whose return to it he would later condemn. His own ideal and goal in this philosophical stage of his development was a life of scholarly retirement and prayer, as we can see from the letters he wrote to like-minded friends just before and after baptism. One of these went to Zenobius, a Neoplatonist in the Theodore-Simplician circle, to whom he dedicated his early dialogue *De Ordine*. (It should be noted that he never dedicated a work to Ambrose.) He knew Zenobius would agree with his removal from the sensory life:

> It is entirely settled between us; I believe that nothing registered by our physical senses can remain what it is even for a split second, but it slips away, flows off, and cannot be fixed in a present state—that is, to put it in the common language, it has no real existence. So the true and heavenly philosophy instructs us to rein in and drug the evil and destructive love of such things, so that the soul, even while still in the body, may be borne up and aspire to what remains the same and is not dispersed by passing appeals.[12]

To his old friend Nebridius he wrote, two years after his baptism, that preparing to die is the priority in life—and how can church leaders, immersed in administrative affairs, do that? There is clearly a shot at Ambrose in this passage:

> God has given to only a few, who he wants to govern church affairs, not only to look for death bravely but eagerly to long for it, and to bear the burden of these duties with

equanimity. But for those who are swept toward such tasks by desire for worldly power, and for those who, while still in private life, seek public activity, I doubt that they are granted the great boon of that readiness for death that we are seeking, in the midst of the clank and clutter and scurrying, when they might have deified themselves [*deificari*] in retirement. If I am wrong in this, I am the dumbest and dullest of men, for I cannot savor and cling to the true good but in safe retirement. A full retreat from the tumult of transitory things is necessary, believe me, for a man to face death without fear, neither oblivious of it nor overconfident, neither itching for easy glory nor cowering in submissive delusion. (*Epistulae* 10)

The breathtaking ambition of Augustine at this point—to become "deified" in this life—comes out in his letter to one Hermogenian, where he separates himself and his friend from the common herd of people Ambrose sought to impress and control.

I think we make enough concession to our times if any pure stream of Plotinus is channeled through dark and thorny tangles, so as to refresh a few, rather than that it be loosed indiscriminately in the open, where its purity cannot be preserved from the random tramplings of cattle. (*Epistulae* 1)

The Augustine of this baptismal period is a far different man from the pastoral figure of a later decade. It was only when he became a bishop himself that he began to see some of the merits of Ambrose.

Ambrose and Augustine were never farther apart than in the late spring and summer of 386, when each was at the height of a personal crisis. Ambrose's drama was public—his struggle with the imperial court over possession of his churches and the spectacular discovery and installation of the relics of Gervase and Protase. Augustine's drama was private, the final effort to give up sexual satisfaction and pledge himself to a life of celibacy. This latter struggle is usually called his "conversion," and it is the most famous scene in *Confessions*. But he was not struggling with intellectual issues. His problem was one of choice, of the resolution to change his life. These are the "seethings" he wanted to consult Ambrose about, but could not, and which he revealed to Simplician. He knew what he should do but felt unable to do it:

> So sick was I, so tortured, as I reviled myself more than ever, churning and chafing in my chains, not broken free of them entirely, held more loosely now but still held, as you were working in my hidden place, with your fierce pity wielding the double whip of fear and shame to prevent my relapse, to prevent the lessening and lighter bond that still held me from strengthening its grip, to grapple me again more tightly than before. My inner self was urging me: Now is the time! Now! With those words I was moving toward a resolution, I was almost there—but was not there. Still, I did not slide all the way back, but braced myself nearby, getting my wind back; then, renewing the effort, I was almost there—almost—and just touched, just grasped the prize. But no, I was not there, I touched not, grasped not, not being ready to let death die in me so life might live in me, my ingrained evil thwarting my untrained good. The moment when I would become someone different, the moment, the closer it came, the more terror it struck in me. (C 8.25)

Then, in the garden where he was struggling, he heard a child's voice saying "Lift! Look!" This made him pick up Paul's

Letter to the Romans, where he read, "Give up indulgence and drunkenness, give up lust and obscenity, give up strife and rivalries, and clothe yourself in Jesus Christ the Lord, leaving no further allowance for fleshly desires" (13.13–14). Augustine had been reading the letters of Paul when Pontician told him about people taking up the ascetic life (C 8.14). He had clearly been reading Paul regularly, perhaps at the urging of Simplician. (We know that he asked Ambrose for later reading, as if he had no guidance before, and we know that Ambrose advised Old Testament readings for catechumens, not the New Testament.) At any rate, this moment resolved his struggle with his will, and he determined to accept baptism and become a celibate. He did not rush to tell Ambrose this, but wrote him later, applying for baptism from the villa at Cassiciacum where he went to write his earliest surviving dialogues about the learned life of a Christian.

Having assessed in this chapter the many ways in which Ambrose did not convert Augustine, or even impress him, it is time to look at the real impact that the older man did have on the petitioner for baptism. It was not Neoplatonism as such that Ambrose could impart to Augustine but the Platonist allegorizing of the Jewish scriptures that was at the core of Ambrose's instruction on the meaning of baptism. Augustine would have six weeks of intense daily indoctrination in this method, and that left a lasting mark on all his later readings of the Bible. It is time to proceed with Augustine toward the font.

PART II

THE
BAPTISM

AUGUSTINE APPROACHES THE FONT

Augustine took his first step toward baptism before he could take any physical steps at all, when he was carried as an infant by his mother to be blessed as a hearer (catechumen) in the church of Tagaste. His mother, Monnica, had to take him there, since she was his only baptized parent. His father, Patrick, was a catechumen himself until baptism late in his life (C 9.22). At the church, Augustine had the sign of the cross made over him, signifying that he had a Christian destiny, and he was anointed with salt as a spiritual preservative. "I was signed already with his cross, seasoned with his salt, when I left the womb of my mother" (C 1.17). As a catechumen, he could later attend church and hear the homilies preached there, though he had to leave before the Eucharistic celebration. Like most hearers, including his father and Ambrose, he was expected to put off baptism till he had sown all his wild oats, since serious sins committed after baptism called for expulsion from the community, with readmission possible only after a demanding public penance (of the sort Emperor Theodosius would undergo after being excommunicated by Ambrose).

While still a boy, Augustine tried to skip the preliminaries and receive an emergency baptism. The ordinary procedure was that all baptisms took place in the Easter season, with an intense Lenten preparation and a course of postbaptismal instruction, all applicants receiving their baptism together. But if death were felt to be imminent, for a child or an adult, a rushed individual baptism could take place. If illness or infancy made the normal immersion impossible, the baptism could be by "aspersion," a pouring of water over the baptizand (the method that became standard in the Middle Ages). That is what Augustine clamored for. "I, while still a boy, almost died from a sudden attack of chest fever"—an ailment that would recur throughout his life—and "I begged for baptism in Christ your son" (C 1.17). At first Monnica agreed to this. "She made quick arrangements for the rites of my ablution in the saving mysteries, with my testimony to you, Lord Jesus, for forgiveness of my sins" (C 1.17).

But when he suddenly recovered, Monnica thought it unsafe for him to face adolescence with its temptations after the one-time forgiveness of baptism. This is one of the things for which Augustine, as bishop, rebukes his dead mother.[1] Like Ambrose, he became a later critic of delayed baptism:

> Why even now is it everywhere dinned into our ears, when this or that class of men is discussed, that we should "Let him carry on, since he is not yet baptized," when we do not say about physical health, "Let him further damage his body, since he is not yet given his health." How much better would it have been for me to be healed on the spot, so that care might be taken of myself by me and by mine, that the healing given my soul should be preserved in your preserving ways who gave it—how much better, indeed. But mighty storm waves, and many, were foreseen rolling over me after childhood, and my mother, understanding this,

preferred to commit to the waters' workings my unshaped
clay rather than a self already reshaped. (C 1.18)

Finally, in 387, at age thirty-five, Augustine was ready to
move from the status of hearer to that of applicant (competens).
From his borrowed villa at Cassiciacum he sent Ambrose a notice
of his intent, asking for reading that might help him prepare
(C 9.13). Since competentes were asked to enroll for baptism at
the feast of the Epiphany, Augustine and his large company had to
head back to Milan in January—which explains why Alypius,
walking barefoot as penitential preparation for his baptism, trod
over icy ground (C 9.14). He had good reason to toughen himself.
Those who entered Lent as competentes faced a grueling course of
training—beginning with a long fast and with abstinence from all
sexual activity, training that Ambrose compared to the condi-
tioning of an athlete, to make them worthy of baptism at the end
of Lent.[2] Every week there would be a physical inspection (scrutamen) combined with an exorcism to rid the body of any diabolical
traces.[3] "By exorcism the sanctifying of the soul as well as the body
is enquired into and established."[4]

Exorcism was a constantly needed and performed ceremony
in the church of the time. In third century Rome, there were 154
clergy, of whom fifty-two were exorcists.[5] The air of late antiquity
was thick with swarming "demons" (daimones), including all the
pagan gods, who were devils in disguise. Fighting off the hold of
these ancient gods and their ceremonies was a principal task of the
exorcists. As Peter Brown says:

> Exorcism, for instance, was a well-known form of religious
> drama. . . . Christians used this common practice to teach
> nothing less than a condensed lesson in the direction of
> world history. Christ, they believed, had already broken
> the power of the demons in the invisible world. Now his

servants could be seen to drive them from their last hiding places on earth. Exorcism rendered palpable the preordained retreat of the gods.[6]

Since those seeking baptism after the last Easter season were getting their first chance at it now, one might expect the gathering at Epiphany to be fairly large. But we do not know how many eligible catechumens were still delaying till their sinful days were over. At any rate, Ambrose once complained about the small number applying at Epiphany—he said he felt like the Apostles working all night and catching no fish.[7] But Augustine and his friends seem to have been ready to get back to Milan by Epiphany. When they turned in their names as applicants, Ambrose said this was equivalent to rubbing mud on their eyes, alluding to the way Jesus rubbed mud on the eyes of the blind man, then told him to go wash it off in the pool at Siloam, at which point his vision was granted him (John 9.6–11). The applicants' mud, a way of confessing their sinful state, would be washed off in the baptismal font (S 3.12).

Ambrose began Lent with a sermon on Elias as the patron of fasts. Ambrose would use only Jewish patriarchs and Solomon's writings as his subjects during the pre-baptismal instructions, as a way of recreating the way God prepared mankind for the coming of Jesus through the Jewish revelations (M1). He was also observing the *disciplina arcani*, the code of silence, which dictated that the full meaning of the faith could be revealed only by those initiated into its mysteries. This, clearly, is why Ambrose urged Augustine to prepare himself by reading Isaiah, a suggestion that left Augustine cold (C 9.13).

Ambrose argues, in his opening sermon, that Elias prepared himself for his great works by a forty-day fast (1 Kings 19.8).[8] Indeed, all the feats of the patriarchs are said to have been enabled by their fasting—a symbol of the fact that fasts prepare one for the life of heaven.

Fasting is the teacher of self-control, the instiller of purity, the humbler of thought, the punisher of the flesh, the conditioner of soberness, the ruler of virtue, the purifier of the soul, the promoter of compassion, the founder of gentleness, the wooer of charity, the adorner of age, the protector of youth—fasting is the soother of difficulties and the nourisher of well-being.[9]

This sermon may have been preached to the whole congregation, telling them to fast throughout Lent except on Saturdays and Sundays. But it had special meaning for the competentes, whose fast would be supplemented with other ordeals. "The Pasch of the Lord concludes the fast—the day of the Resurrection, when the chosen ones are baptized."[10] Indeed, Elias is made a forerunner of the grace of baptism, since when the heavens were closed to punish Ahab, it was Elias who opened them (1 Kings 18.42–45):

Elias showed the type of baptism by opening heaven, which had been shut for three years and six months. Far greater are the fulfillments of that type. For it was not descending rain that opened heaven but ascending grace, since no one rises to the kingdom of heaven but by water along with grace. It was unbelief that shut heaven against men, but belief that opened it. Once before heaven opened to mankind, when Enoch was carried up to heaven. Then it was shut again, till Elias opened it, and he was carried up in a chariot. So you will be able to rise up if you seek the favor of the sacrament.[11]

Here began Augustine's deep exposure to Ambrose's method of reading Jewish scripture, as foreshadowing the Christian "mysteries." The Elias story was clearly tailored to the situation of the applicants, telling them how to think of the baptism they were about to receive. The competentes probably heard this sermon along with the regular attendants at Mass, which they were allowed to witness though they had to leave before the Eucharistic service. During the rest of Lent, they would be taught, twice a day, in a special place reserved for their instruction.

Where was that place? It has been assumed by some that the competentes left the Basilica Vetus to reassemble in the baptistry. But Ambrose speaks of their seeing the interior of the baptistry for the first time on the day of their immersion, and he describes its interior as first revealed on that occasion. The baptistry was opened only on Easter (G 4), otherwise it was kept as "the holy of holies," like the inner Temple the high priest could enter only once a year. On the occasion (Palm Sunday, 386) when the emperor's troops interrupted Ambrose at Mass, he says that he took the competentes out of the Basilica Vetus to teach them the creed *in baptisterii basilica*, "in the church of the baptistry" (*Epistulae* 76.4). Normally he calls the baptistry just *baptisterium*. What could be the *church* of the baptistry? Would he take them out of the Basilica Vetus into the Basilica Nova? But that was being prepared for their entry on Easter, for their first Eucharist, and it would soon be occupied by the emperor's troops. Since *basilica* could mean any church building in the fourth century (we have seen that Ambrose had several basilicas outside the walls of Milan), this seems to mean some separate ecclesiastical property connected to the function of the baptistry, what some have later called a catechumeneum, a secluded teaching place where the competentes could receive their twice-daily instructions and their weekly physical inspections, and perhaps conduct special prayer meetings. It would be a halfway house reflecting their condition as not fully part of the regular congregation yet having their own special status.

We are fortunate in possessing Ambrose's instructions on the patriarchs that were delivered during the Lenten preaching to the competentes. He says that he concentrated for this purpose on the patriarchs and what he took to be the writings of Solomon (the Song of Songs, Ecclesiastes, and Proverbs). He concentrated on four main patriarchs, each to inculcate a specific virtue.

> In Joseph there was a special incandescence of chastity . . .
> [just as] in Abraham you have learned the fierce adherence
>   to faith,
> in Isaac the purity of a single intent,
> in Jacob a special resilience under harsh test.[12]

He thought concrete examples taken from the patriarchs were more useful than abstract teachings, whether philosophical maxims or theological doctrines. "Though precepts are more general, examples are more applicable, and they soak into the mind better the more pointed and specific they are" (De Joseph 1.1).

The treatments of the patriarchs that have reached us in written form come from the period of Augustine's baptism (the 380s). They reflect approximately, and perhaps exactly, what was said in 387.[13] At any rate, they reflect what Ambrose tailored to the specific needs of competentes. The bishop had been conducting these sessions for thirteen years by 387, and they clearly distill his experience in this kind of instruction. There is a baptismal aspect to what he says about each patriarch. He takes them up in chronological order, passing in each case from father to son. There was plenty of material to fill up the forty days of teaching, with biblical history and the practical and mystical writings of Solomon. Since Sundays do not count in the forty fasting days of Lent (which actually extends for forty-six days), and Ambrose might have omitted Saturdays as well, that leaves thirty week days for teaching—which means Ambrose held sixty sessions of instruction for his Applicants.

Abraham

This first treatment of a patriarch lays the groundwork for all the ones that follow by arguing that the biblical accounts are better than pagan presentations of an ideal. Unlike the imaginary city of Plato's *Republic* or the idealized rule of Xenophon's *Cyropaedia*, the patriarchs are real historical figures (*De Abraham* 1.2.2).[14] That means that they have faults which bring them closer to people who want to imitate their virtues. Of Abraham he writes: "I have affirmed from the outset that his mind needed shaping, since from the outset it was not finished, but needed improvement by gradual stages" (2.6.26). Apart from personal failings, the patriarchs suffer from living under different rules in their historical context. That is something Ambrose has to face for all the patriarchs, who were allowed sexual liberties forbidden to the baptismal applicants being addressed by Ambrose—polygamy, concubinage, prostitution, even (in Lot's case) incest. Ambrose takes two tacks with regard to these potentially unedifying events. First, he argues that the patriarchs lived before the Law was given to Moses, so they could not observe what they knew nothing about (1.4.23). Second, in each case there were special circumstances. Abraham had to take a concubine, since Sarah was sterile in their early marriage, and his line had to continue for the good of the whole human race. Lot's daughters had to sleep with him because they thought he was the sole surviving human, and even then they had to get him drunk for him to agree to sleep with them (1.6.54–58). Abraham only took Hagar to bed at Sarah's bidding, for the sake of offspring: "The excuse of political duty (*publici muneris gratia*) covered up individual defect (*privatam culpam*)" (1.4.24).

Furthermore, the patriarchs were led to acts which are prefigurations of the history of salvation. Abraham sees that he must put away Hagar and her son, since she is a type of the synagogue, and he must cleave to Sarah and her son, since they are types of the church (1.4.26). The competentes had to learn the lesson of the typology without claiming the license given to patriarchs. They could not even take advantage of the Roman law of their time that permits concubinage, divorce, and sex with slave women. They entered a new moral realm through the waters of baptism, one in which men are held to the same requirement of chastity as women (1.4.25). As Abraham committed adultery before the Law was given, so the competentes may have sinned before their baptism.

> Did you sin while outside the church (*gentilis*)? You have that excuse. But now you have come to the church, and you hear the rule: You shall not commit adultery. You no longer have an excuse. Because I am speaking to those who have given in their names for baptism, if anyone has committed this sin, let him know that he is forgiven, but only as one who has committed the sin but knows he must not do so any more. Just as the adulteress condemned by the pharisaical scribes was forgiven by the Lord—who then said, "Go and see that you sin no more." What he says to her he says to you. Did you sin when outside the church? Did you sin as a catechumen? It is forgiven; your sin is removed by baptism. Go and see that after this you sin no more. You have used up your excuse from Abraham. (1.4.23)

Ambrose argues that the patriarchs strove for the concept of chastity available to them, and they show the competentes that they, with the help of a higher law and the graces about to be given them in baptism, can reach that previously unrealized goal. "You who aspire to baptism and to wear the white robe of the faith, learn the lesson of continence" (1.7.59)

Abraham is above all a model of faith. He has to rely on the Lord's guidance, from the time when he leaves Egypt (2.8.49) to the time when he agrees to sacrifice his only son Isaac. He believes that God has a purpose in ordering this sacrifice, though he does not know what it is. Ambrose says that his *competentes* know it now—that Abraham was foreshadowing the Father's sacrifice of his only Son, Jesus (1.8.72–78). All that Abraham knew was that if God ordered it, good would somehow come of it.

But how was Abraham to know that God had ordered it? Ambrose does not defend a blind faith. That is why he presents Abraham as a hero not only of faith but of natural knowledge as well (2.1.1–4). Marcia Colish argues that the hunt for Neoplatonism in Ambrose has led people to overlook the fact that his teaching on the patriarchs, like his greatest statement on morals, *De Officiis* (The conduct of clergy), has a firm Aristotelian and Stoic foundation.[15] Unlike the Neoplatonists, who divided soul from body, Ambrose is a hylomorphist: "What then is man? Soul, or body, or a union of the two? We are one thing, our possessions another" (*De Isaac vel Anima* 2.3).[16] Like Aristotle, he sees the soul as the form of the body: "The soul animates and governs the otherwise insensate and inanimate body" (2.4). Thus Abraham judges with a refined reason, foreswearing superstitions like astrology (*De Abraham* 2.3.8–9). This part of the treatise would have special meaning for Augustine, who was once enamored of astrology and parted from it with difficulty (C 4.46).

Another thing that would strike Augustine is the heavy use of typology in *De Abraham*. Note, for instance, all the animal symbolism. The animals Abraham is ordered to sacrifice are "mystical figures"—the calf of our bodily flesh, the goat of our senses, and the ram of our speech (2.8.50–51). This leads Ambrose to the visionary animals seen by Ezekiel, the man, the lion, the ox, and the eagle (2.8.54). These are often taken by Christians (including Augustine) as types of the four gospels. But Ambrose takes them, in the first place, as elements of the soul—reason (the man), courage (the lion), desire (the ox), and vision (the eagle). This is the kind of symbolism Augustine would become adept at.

Isaac

Ambrose deprived himself of the most dramatic material in Isaac's story, since he had already told that tale in his instruction on Abraham. That meant that he had to go straight for typology, neglecting the historical background. He begins by making the connection between Isaac and Jesus, "the one presented, the other prefigured" (*De Isaac vel Anima* 1.1). Both Isaac and Jesus were born miraculously (Isaac to an ancient woman long sterile, Jesus to a virgin); both were called to save their people; both were offered in sacrifice; both were saved from death, Isaac by an angelic intervention, Jesus by resurrection. Ambrose connects the three wells Isaac dug with Jesus's meeting the Samaritan woman by the well, and to baptism's "fountain of living water" (1.2, 4.25). In a further refinement, he sees Isaac's three wells as the three sources of wisdom in the writings of Solomon—moral wisdom in Proverbs, natural wisdom in Ecclesiastes, and mystical wisdom in the Song of Songs (4.23).

Since Isaac is the type of Christ, his wife, Rebecca, becomes a type of the church, drawn to Christ by love and obedience. The bulk of the treatise concerns her (and the applicants') education in the three forms of knowledge represented by the wells. But the predominant knowledge to be gained is mystical, worked out in an elaborate comparison of the soul's attraction to Christ with the lover's approach to the bridegroom in the Song of Songs. By the end of this treatise, Rebecca has been reborn in the crucible of love—compared to the immersion of baptism (8.76)—and she manages the steeds of what his text of the Song of Songs called "the chariot of Aminadab" (Song of Songs 6.12). In Ambrose's reading, this chariot of the soul has eight horses drawing it, four of them obedient (prudence, temperance, fortitude, justice) and four of them unruly (wrath, lust, fear, injustice). The essentially Stoic task of Rebecca is not to eliminate the unruly elements but to control them, make them run with their tamer yokemates (8.65). It is the assignment Ambrose has also given his applicants.

Jacob

In Ambrose's summary of the patriarchs' leading virtues at *De Joseph* 1.1, Jacob was said to have "a special resilience under harsh trials." So the first part of the treatise devoted to him portrays the equanimity of the ideal Stoic:

> The sage, you see, is neither shattered by blows to his body nor bewildered by setbacks. He remains serene amid afflictions. Bodily torments do not lessen the working of his happiness or sour its enjoyment. For the happy life is not derived from the body's pleasures but from the awareness that one bears no taint of sin, from mental recognition that happiness lies in what is good, even if painful—not in what is wrong, even if sweet. The origin of the good life is not ease of body but alertness of mind. (*De Jacob* 1.7.27–28)[17]

Ambrose has a special difficulty in this treatise, arising from what preceded it. In the *De Isaac*, Rebecca was a model of spiritual growth and maturity. But here she helps the younger son, Jacob, cheat the older one, Esau, out of his birthright. Ambrose has to do some special pleading for his heroine. On the one hand, he admits that parents should be impartial in favoring all their children. But he also claims:

> There is a certain healthy rivalry [*bonum certamen*] in parental concerns, the mother focusing on love, the father on merit. The mother's affection favors the younger child; the father's sense of natural precedence favors the elder.

One honors more; the other loves more. Both parents favor both children, so long as they do not combine to support one and deprive the other. Let favor be equally dispersed by the contending emphases, so that parental love dispensed is balanced out, one parent paying more when the other comes short. (2.1.7)

The commercial imagery, typical of Ambrose, is in the Latin: *compenset . . . imminuit*. We are reminded in passages like this that Ambrose began his life as a legal advocate. The case he makes cannot cover up the fact that Rebecca deceived Isaac in disguising one son as the other, to take away what was the other's right. So Ambrose resorts again to typology. Esau had to be rejected because he was a type of the synagogue, as Jacob had to be promoted as a type of the church (2.29). Indeed, the hairy disguise Jacob wore was a priestly cloak rightly worn by prophets. Besides, the Lord's pronouncement (*oraculum*) was that the younger one should rule the elder (2.2.8). Thus Rebecca, in praying over her choice, did not so much "put down the first brother for the second as offer up the second to the Lord," since "with this devout mother, the divine portent [*mysterium*] was trumping [*praeponderabat*] a family bond [*pignus*]" (2.2.6). Augustine would later argue for God's predestinating will from this favoring of Jacob over Esau.[18]

In a similar way, Jacob's tricky way of insuring that he would get the striped lambs Laban guaranteed to his lot—by placing parti-colored trees in their sight as they copulated—is explained by making the three kinds of trees symbolic of the Trinity. The storax stood for the Father, since it can render incense to him. The walnut is a sign of the Son, since Aaron bore it, flowering, as a priestly emblem. The plane tree is for the Holy Spirit, since it supports vines so well (2.4.19). Ambrose is on dangerous ground. To save the sacred text, he has to distinguish "holy cheating" (*pia fraus*, 2.4.10) from things like the dirty tricks played on Jacob by Laban.

"Deception is allowed [*bonus dolus*] when it seizes a thing innocently, since 'from the time of John the kingdom of the heavens is being enforced, and the enforcers seize it' [Matthew 11.12]."

Another defense of deception (*dolus*) is cleverly turned into a description of what the competentes will undergo at the font. Jacob's wife Rachel has stolen the household gods of her father Laban. When they are searched for, she hides them by sitting on the saddlebags that hold them (2.5.25). Ambrose says it was right to steal the false gods—Jacob buried them under a sterile tree, as a sign that the old ways must die: "Every error of the pagans is truly buried whenever one is washed clean of vices. Our old man, once nailed to the cross, forgets being a slave to sin . . . [and] all those baptized in Christ are buried with him" (2.7.34).

Toward the end of his *De Jacob*, Ambrose switches to a long description of the deaths of the Maccabees, so suddenly that scholars have wondered why. He makes an awkward transition, saying that Jacob remained happy despite sufferings because of his firm grasp on basic reality, which leads him to the topos of martyrs remaining serene under torture. In a sudden dramatic stroke, he appeals to the Maccabee martyr-priest Eleazar to pray for him, as if *he*, Ambrose, were now facing martyrdom (2.10.43). Continuing his dramatic reliving of events, he puts words in the mouth of Antiochus IV, the Seleucid king who killed Eleazar, as he tried to persuade him to save his life by giving up his religion (he had been asked to eat pork). Then he quotes Eleazar's stirring refusal of the offer of life: "I am not so old that courage has failed to stay young in me!" (2.10.43). This is followed by circumstantial accounts of the execution of the seven Maccabee sons of a brave mother.

Ambrose draws mainly on the apocryphal Fourth Book of Maccabees, written by Pseudo-Josephus, which is itself full of Stoic rhetoric and pious bravado from each son. Their deaths are presented as a crescendo of ever more horrible butchery, going from the oldest son to the youngest, since Antiochus hoped that each slaughter would break the following victim. One is flayed alive, another broken on a wheel, another burnt to death, another torn to pieces. When all seven of them have died bravely, defying the torturer, their mother is at last killed. For Ambrose, of course, her number as the eighth to die has a special meaning—the sons died like the seven days of the week, and she is the exemplar outside the ordinary order (2.11.53). Eight, as he said in explaining the baptistry's octagonal form, was the sign of eternity.

Ambrose always glorified martyrs, though he sometimes said that the age of martyrs was over (he does not talk that way in this extraordinarily detailed account of gruesome deaths). When he asks Eleazar to pray for him, and then addresses the competentes as if they may have to face suffering for their faith, the work has entered a new key. He describes the solidarity of spirit among the Maccabees, and the way their mother offered them up to the Lord:

> Each cheered the other on and said, with one spirit as in spiritual ranks, "Let us defy death's advance, for we shall live on in death. Let none of us desert the ranks of religion, let none of us miss the triumph of this death...." So no one feared, none cowered, none hesitated, none of the brothers' number drew back from death. .... Their mother, looking on this solidarity in her sons' cohort, offered up her sons as parts of her own body, and it seemed that she underwent their specific tortures in herself. (2.12.55)

It is not surprising that many readers have seen in this whole sequence the way Ambrose urged his flock to stay together when they were under siege from the emperors in Holy Week of 386—when, as Augustine writes, "they were ready to die with their bishop" (C 9.15). In fact, some have tried to date this treatise to 386, so resonant is it with the fears of that time. But Marcia Colish points out that by Holy Week in 386 Ambrose would already have delivered his third Lenten discourse.[19] So the earliest possible date, and clearly the most appropriate one, for recalling and reliving the solidarity with his people under threat would be the next year, 387, the anniversary of the struggle, the year when Augustine was present to hear this extraordinary passage.

Joseph

Ambrose had very warm relations with his older siblings. His sister, the oldest, was the consecrated virgin he celebrated in his book *De Virginibus*, and to whom he wrote some of his most revealing letters. His brother, Satyrus, was the next oldest, and Ambrose resembled him so closely that people mistook them for each other; Satyrus gave up his own political career to manage Ambrose's material needs when he became bishop.[20] The three siblings consulted each other often.[21] I think we can conclude that their parents treated these talented children impartially, which explains why Ambrose is so troubled when he finds the Bible apparently sanctioning favoritism. We saw how he had to come up with a supernatural command to excuse Rebecca's promotion of the younger Jacob over the elder Esau, and he faces the same problem in the story of Joseph. The favoritism of Isaac toward Joseph prompts his other sons to sell Joseph into slavery. Once again, the only excuse Ambrose can think of is that a revelation told Jacob that Joseph was destined to be a savior to other people—another foreshadowing of Christ. "It would seem that he showed preference not as father to son but as prophet to portent [*mysterium*]" (*De Joseph* 2.6).[22]

Both here and in the *De Jacob*, Ambrose goes out of his way to tell his applicants that the exception given to the patriarchs does not apply to them in their own role as parents:

> It is joyful to love one's children, and even more to love them
> generously. But often this very love in a parent, if indulged
> too freely, is harmful to the children, if overindulgence gives

too free rein to a favored child, or if a preference for one drives the others from their sibling affection. A child benefits more if he is allowed to win the love of his brothers. This is a more signal generosity on the parents' part. It is a more rewarding benefaction given the children. Let equal favor bind offspring together, just as equal blood does. True piety does not recognize a material payout with a net loss of love. (2.5)

Once again, the imagery is commercial: *lucrum . . . dispendium*. A noteworthy aspect of these patriarchal discourses is that they are not, like some of his writings, directed to one gender or the other—to male priests or to female consecrated virgins. Most of the competentes are already married or will be in the future. Ambrose's advice to them is markedly practical and down to earth—so much so that Marcia Colish subtitles her book on the discourses *Ethics for the Common Man*. So, in the course of the four treatises, he discusses marital duties; parental responsibility; and practical lessons on generosity, on mutual forgiveness, and on staying within one's means. He counsels the women against undue extravagance in dress or jewelry (*De Abraham* 1.9.87).

Thus, in this discourse, he warns men that they must stick to their word. When Joseph is sent to prison, he helps a fellow prisoner, the Pharaoh's former wine steward, who promises to remember his help when he gets out. But the steward, released and returned to the Pharaoh's court, does not keep his promise, and Ambrose excoriates him to impress upon the competentes the evil of not honoring a commitment (6.34).

When Ambrose was listing the respective principal virtues of his four patriarchs, the one he assigned to Joseph was chastity (1.1). The main reason for that is his repulse of Potiphar's wife when she tries to seduce him (5.23–25). When he turned her down, she claimed that he was the one who made sexual advances to her, which led to his being imprisoned (5.26). Ambrose takes this occasion to tell the applicants that when injustice comes their way, they should bear it with patience as Joseph did (5.26). Later, when the brothers who had betrayed him sought his help after he became a powerful assistant to the pharaoh, he forgave them. Ambrose preaches forgiveness from this episode—there were endless practical lessons to be drawn from the life of Joseph.

Just as the story of the Maccabees in the *De Jacob* referred to the fight over the basilicas, a reference in the *De Joseph* recalls an incident in that struggle. The emperor's powerful eunuch, Calligonus, had threatened Ambrose with death if he did not vacate his cathedral. Ambrose wrote to his sister that he answered: "Should God permit you to succeed in your threat, I shall suffer as becomes a bishop, and you shall act as becomes a eunuch" (*Epistulae* 76.28). Ambrose recalls this incident because Joseph was imprisoned with eunuchs, one of whom he predicted would be executed. Ambrose notes that the eunuch Calligonus was executed in 388, after Valentinian left Milan (6.30). This point could not, of course, be made in the 387 discourses. It may have been inserted in the text after the man's demise.

What did Augustine take from Ambrose's intense and extensive course in how to read the Jewish scripture? Obviously, the typological approach to the Bible was the main benefit, as Augustine noted in his *Confessions*: "Where the literal sense seemed to present absurd things, a symbolic reading opened new meanings behind the veil of mystery" (C 6.6). He was able to watch Ambrose wrestle with difficult problems in the texts. How, for instance, was one to interpret the patriarchal indulgence in polygamy? What could one make of deception and fraud like the theft of Esau's birthright? Could one condone the apparently arbitrary treatment of favored children? No matter how one judged Ambrose's conclusions on all these matters, he showed that it was possible to find deeper meanings behind apparent "absurdity."

There was another lesson that came through the treatment in its totality. The Jewish scripture was presented as continuingly valid and inspired, not as superseded by the New Testament. Ambrose always read the two bodies of scripture in tandem, as complementary. The patriarchs are saints, guided by the Holy Spirit. As he told his audience after their immersion, they had been informed about the patriarchs so they could "take the route of these elders to follow the divine signals" (*M* 1). He equated the slaughtered Maccabees with Christian martyrs. In the book he modeled on Cicero's *De Officiis*, Ambrose substitutes for the heroes of classical antiquity in Cicero's book, the patriarchs and prophets of the Jewish Bible (*O* 26–27). He claimed that the Queen of Sheba learning from Solomon was a type of the church learning from Jesus (*O* 296). Ambrose would have agreed with the Venetians who dedicated Christian churches to Jewish heroes—the churches of "Saint Job," for instance, and "Saint Moses." Indeed, Milan's own Basilica of the Prophets, if not named by Ambrose, certainly honored his view of the Jewish patriarchs and prophets.

Augustine has been singled out by the profound scholar (and Orthodox Jew) Paula Fredriksen as a startling exception among early Christian thinkers in his opposition to the persecution of Jews.[23] It cannot be said that Ambrose took him all the way to his final position on this matter. But he surely gave Augustine much to reflect on when he treated Jewish scripture with such respect in these discourses, asking that the Applicants go deeper into the matter than some Christians, who dismissed the Jewish religion as primitive or no longer of consequence. Like Ambrose, Augustine called the Maccabees martyrs for God (*Epistulae* 40.6).

Ambrose himself was not thoroughly enlightened on the subject of Jews. As we have seen, he justified the rejections of Leah, Esau, Joseph's brothers as types of the synagogue, and he rebuked the emperor Theodosius for making Christians who burned down a synagogue rebuild it. It was not till the 390s, ten years after his baptism, that Augustine transcended such attitudes. This occurred, according to Fredriksen, when Augustine wrote his massive *Contra Faustum Manichaeum.*

Augustine's own mockery of Jewish scripture had grown from his early adoption of Manichean doctrine, which treated that revelation as idiotic. He moved away from that position under the guidance of Ambrose. But only when confronting Faustus did he perceive that his Manichean arguments against the Jewish scripture were the same as those against the New Testament's reliance on the Old Testament, and Augustine moved to defend them both on the grounds that they were both God's message to mankind, and one part of it could not be rejected or suppressed. They made up a "double canon."[24] Jews bore witness to the Lord who chose them, and their witness should in no way be silenced. This was not entirely the teaching of Ambrose, but one wonders if Augustine could have reached his own conclusion without the earlier help from Ambrose.

A final hint from Ambrose's discourses may show up in Augustine's own practice. He presumably saw the usefulness of continued preaching on a single theme in these careful treatments of the patriarchs. Delivered to the applicants in a sustained volley, two a day for thirty days, they had a cumulative effect. With their wide use of both the Jewish and Christian scripture, they showed long contemplation and careful preparation. The same would be true of the cycles of demanding sermons Augustine presented to his flock in Africa. He preached a sermon (sometimes more than one) on all 150 of the Psalms. He preached a cycle of 124 homilies on John's Gospel. These were not given in one unbroken sequence but spaced out over time. But can anyone imagine a modern priest or bishop engaged in such long and careful treatment of the Bible from his pulpit?

Perhaps the closest Augustine came to imitating Ambrose's Easter cycle of instruction was in the ten sermons he preached on the First Epistle of John. Eight of these were delivered during Easter week of 407, when two homilies were given every day.[25] This was a rhythm and a discipline that Ambrose would have been familiar with.

AUGUSTINE AT THE FONT

The Lenten exercises of the applicants reached their first climax on Palm Sunday, when the creed was committed to them. This was not a public document in the early church. It was kept under the code of secrecy (*disciplina arcani*), since it had almost magical properties. Ambrose called the creed "a protection always at hand and a keepsake in our hearts."[1] Still, we have the text of Ambrose's *Explanatio Symboli* (Exposition of the creed), since the creed was called the symbol. *Symbolon* was a Greek word for contract, from *syn* (together) and *ballein* (to put). The parts to be put together are explained this way: "*Symbola* are formed from any physical token divided in two and kept separately by the parties to an agreement or transaction; the two pieces could later be rejoined to verify their fit and so authenticate the origin of a message."[2] Later, in the age of parchment, this kind of contract would be called an indenture, since the parted pieces had "toothmark" edges to be fit together. But papyrus and paper were not tough enough to use that way, so the Greeks broke ostraca or other potterylike substances that could be fitted along their jagged break lines.

Ambrose did not like this Greek etymology for *symbolon*. He preferred a usage that had grown up in the commercial circles that intrigued him, in which *sym-ballein* was used for "putting in" money or other valuables in a common fund, to be used as a guarantor for later activities. The reason Ambrose wanted this meaning was that he accepted the legend that the Apostles' Creed was formed before the apostles went off on their separate missionary journeys (on which they would all be martyred). Each of the twelve apostles "put in" one clause of the twelve articles of the creed, and used the common result wherever he went as the guarantor of orthodoxy. Ambrose compares that to the creation of a credit fund built up for common use.

> First we should take up the meaning of the word itself. "Symbol" is a Greek word for which the Latin is "collection." Businessmen particularly refer to a "symbol" when they chip in money so that, consolidated from their individual contributions, it can be stabilized and kept safe, so no one may tamper with the whole or with a part. With these businessmen, then, it is the rule that anyone tampering with the funds is expelled as a thief. (2)

Ambrose creates an analogy by which anyone tampering with the creed—the common fund of doctrine—is expelled as a heretic (7).

Ambrose listed the twelve articles in three groups of four (the divisions indicated in our text, but not spelled out because of the *disciplina arcani*). This shows that he broke down the creed this way:

1. I believe in God the Father Almighty
2. And in Jesus Christ, his only Son, our Lord

3. Who was born of the Holy Spirit from the virgin Mary
4. Who suffered under Pontius Pilate, died, and was buried.
1. On the third day he rose again from the dead;
2. He ascended into heaven
3. And sits at the right hand of the Father,
4. Whence he shall come again to judge the living and the dead.
1. I believe in the Holy Spirit,
2. The holy Catholic Church,
3. The forgiveness of sins
4. And the resurrection of the body. (8)

This division was meant to make it easier for the competentes to memorize it.

On Palm Sunday, in their catechumencum, the applicants were asked to sign themselves with the cross, to dedicate them to what would follow, and then the symbol was read (3). After a brief explanation, stressing the three separate persons of the Trinity, the group recited the symbol a first time. Then Ambrose went into greater detail, showing how the symbol refutes various heresies—Patripassionists, Sabellians, Arians (4). After this Ambrose explained the symbol clause by clause, giving a brief comment after each clause was recited (5–6). Then the applicants crossed themselves again and recited the clauses in groups of four (perhaps antiphonally), repetition driving the clauses into memory

> I want you to be well aware of this, that the symbol should not be written down. For you to have it always at hand, let no one write it. Why is that? We have received it on condition that it not be written. Again, why? To keep it. You say, "How keep it if it is not written?" It is better kept if unwritten. How is that true? Here is why. When you write something, you are confident you can retrieve it and you do not keep recalling it by daily meditation. When you do not

write it, however, you worry that you may lose it, and daily you keep recalling it. That is a great safeguard. When lethargy of mind or body comes along, or trial from an enemy (which is never lacking), some trembling of the body, some queasiness of the stomach, just recall the symbol and have a cure. But recall it deep within—and why? So you do not fall into the habit of speaking it aloud before others and thereby slip into speaking it before catechumens or heretics. (9)

Having impressed on the competentes the significance and privilege of safeguarding the creed (and being safeguarded by it), Ambrose was ready, in six more days, to begin the final rites.

The climax of all these preparations came on Easter morning. This was a time of great change and renewal for the whole church community. Easter morning was when the congregation went in procession out from the Basilica Vetus, where the principal liturgy had been celebrated since the end of October, into the Basilica Nova, which would be the center of Ambrose's faithful people throughout the Easter season and the entire summer.[3] We are not told how the baptismal ceremony was integrated into this grand event, but since the baptism took place at the earliest dawn, the neophytes in their "snow white" garb probably led the procession, after they had been baptized, from one basilica to the other, as living symbols of the resurrection from the healing waters.

But first they had to undergo their baptism in the privacy of the baptistry, whose interior they would see for the first time as dawn broke over Milan (G 4). They gathered, either in their catechumeneum or at the baptistry door, for a preliminary ritual of "opening." Ambrose said to each in turn "Effetha," drawing on Mark 7.33–35, where Jesus cures a deaf-mute. Taking his own saliva and touching the man's tongue, he says "Ephphatha" ("Be opened" in Aramaic, the language of Jesus' followers). Ambrose touched the ears "so they may open up to the words and counsel of the bishop" (S 1.2). He did not touch the tongue, since he said it was inappropriate for a man to do so with a woman. Instead, he touched the nostrils, "so you may inhale the fine odor of everlasting reverence, and say, 'We are Christ's incense offered to the Father,' as the holy Apostle said [2 Corinthians 2.15], and there may be in you all the perfumes of belief and devotion" (S 1.3).

After this, the applicants were admitted to the baptistry—men and women probably in separate groups, either successively or in the two baptistries (one connected to the Vetus, the other to the Nova).[4] In any case, Ambrose had to preside over both groups. As an entry rite, the applicants first faced west to renounce the devil, turning toward the place where the sun sets (M 7). They were questioned by Ambrose (M 2):

> When [the bishop] asked, "Do you renounce the devil and his works?" what did you answer? "I renounce them." "Do you renounce the world and its pleasures?" what did you answer? "I renounce them." Remember your pledge, and do not let the sequence of your commitment escape you. If you sign a bond you are held liable for money received and you are accountable to the holder of the bond, whether you like it or not. If you resist you go to court and you are held to your commitment. (S 1.2.5)

One of the fascinating things about Ambrose is the way he combines mystical rites with commercial transactions.

After the renunciation of the devil, applicants turned to the east, to the arriving sun (and returning Christ), and professed their acceptance of the Lord. "After facing west, to perceive your adversary, whom you intend renouncing to his face, you turned about to the east; for whoever renounces the devil is turned to Christ and sees him in immediate focus" (M 7).

Then the applicants removed their clothes, in the niches of the baptistry, in preparation for immersion in the pool. Nudity in a church service may seem odd to us, but we should remember that Milanese of that day were used to public nudity in the baths.[5] Indeed, it is likely that the competentes all went to the public baths before their weekly inspections. And they probably went there on the Saturday before Easter, to have as perfect a body as possible for the ceremony. Peter Brown says that public nudity was actually a sign of privilege:

> Nudity and sexual shame were questions of social status: the way people felt about being naked, or seeing others naked, depended to a large extent on their social situation. Thus, at the top of society, nudity in the public baths expressed the utter ease of the well-to-do, moving without a trace of sexual shame in front of their inferiors.[6]

Vulnerability to sexual exploitation was a matter of the lower classes, which the church fought by applying to all the same privilege that had favored the aristocracy.

The connection of baptism with public baths is suggested in a famous passage of Augustine's *Confessions*: "When my father saw in the public baths that my childhood was gone and I was clothed with unstable young manhood [*inquieta indutum adulescentia*], he mentioned it to my mother, overjoyed with anticipation of having grandchildren by me" (C 2.6). The odd word in that passage is "clothed." He was nude in the baths yet he says he was *clothed*—clothed with unstable [*inquieta*] young manhood. *Inquietum cor*—unstable heart—is perhaps the most famous phrase in the *Confessions* ("Our hearts are unstable until stabilized in you," C 1.1). The father's inspection of him was like the *scrutamina* the applicants underwent. But in the baptistry Augustine would end up "clothed in Christ," following the injunction of Paul, "Be clothed [*induite*] in Christ Jesus" (Romans 13.14). This is the very text Augustine opens at the crucial moment when he surrenders to God in the garden (C 8.29).

Adam before the fall was naked, but Augustine says he wore the "clothing" [*indutamentum*] of innocence (*The City of God* 14.17). Only after the fall did he have to clothe himself in fig leaves. Augustine, thinking in theological symbols, contrasts the physical bath that does not bring grace and salvation, along with a worldly father who thinks only of succession in this life, with the immersion he will undergo in the baptistry, where Ambrose is the father and eternal life is at stake.

When the baptizands were stripped, priests and deacons oiled their bodies as an athlete's body is oiled (G 105–6).

> You were anointed as an athlete of Christ, as going to fight the fight against this world. You stated the issues of your fight. The wrestler has something he aspires to. Where the match is, there is a crown. . . . You are wrestling with the world, to be crowned by Christ. And the crown is for struggling with the world. For though the prize is in heaven, yet winning it takes place here. (S 1.2)

Then Ambrose blessed the water in the font, exorcising it of all impurities (G 88–89).

> The water must be blessed before the one to be baptized enters it. Beforehand, the bishop exorcises the material substance of water. Then he offers a dedication and prayer that the water may be sanctified and the eternal Trinity enter it. Christ first descends [here Ambrose dipped the crucifix in the water, M 14] and then the Spirit. Why in this order? It is so that Christ may not be seen as needing the secret workings [*mysterium*] of sanctification but may sanctify it himself, as the Spirit also does. That is what happened when Christ was baptized, and only then the Holy Spirit descended in appearance like a dove, and the

Father, God, also spoke from heaven [Matthew 3.16]. So the entire Trinity is present in the water. (S 1.18–19)

Now, one by one, each baptizand went down the steps into the water, conducted by Ambrose, a priest, and deacons (S 2.16). Standing waist deep in the pool, each had his or her head dunked under the water three times.

> You were asked, "Do you believe in God the all-powerful?" You answered, "I believe." And you were submerged [*mersisti*]–that is, you were buried.
>
> Again you were asked, "Do you believe in our Lord Jesus Christ and in his cross?" You said, "I believe." And you were submerged—meaning you were buried with Christ. For whoever is buried with Christ rises with Christ.
>
> You were asked a third question, "Do you believe in the Holy Spirit?" You said, "I believe," that this threefold profession might absolve you of the multiple downfalls of your former life. (S 2.20)

The Ambrosian rite, unlike others of the time, inserted "and in his cross" before the second immersion, showing the stress Ambrose laid on the crucifix in the ceremony—along with repeated references to being baptized "in blood and water." The reference to the baptizand's "*multiple* downfalls" in the comment on the third immersion prompts Ambrose to connect the threefold "I believe" with Peter's repentance for his triple denial of Christ and his answer to Christ's thrice-repeated question "Do you love me?" (S 2.21, quoting John 21.15–17).

When the baptizands come from the water, Ambrose says, it is like Christ coming from the tomb: "Since baptism is like death, surely when you are submerged and reemerge this is like a resurrection" (S 3.2). Some think that the postbaptismal anointing of the head took place immediately as the baptizands left the pool. But that could happen only after Ambrose brought all in the company to the other side. Then he had to put his own clothes back on.

We should remember that April in Milan can be chilly in the morning, especially in a building normally closed all winter. It seems clear that the baptizands—now officially neophytes (new-born)—must have put on the clothes they would wear under their white robes (ceremonially bestowed later on) before the anointing and foot washing got under way.

The anointing beforehand was of the whole body, which would be washed in the pool. That afterwards is only of the head.

> You receive myrrh, "ointment for the head [Psalms 133.2]." Why for the head? Because "the perception of a wise man is in his head," as Solomon [Ecclesiastes 2.14] says. Wisdom without favor is sapless, but when wisdom is joined with favor, its operation begins to reach completion. This is the story of rebirth. (S 3.1)

Ambrose gives us the exact words he said as he anointed each person: "May God, the Father all-powerful, who has given you rebirth from water and the Holy Spirit and forgiven your sins, anoint you for eternal life" (S 2.224).

Ambrose then began, and priests carried on, the washing of each neophyte's feet (S 3.4). This was not done in other churches. Ambrose singles out Rome as not following the practice—he suggests that it may have so many baptisms as to make the act cumbersome (S 3.5). Ambrose had a peculiar reason for insisting on the washing, one that Augustine would not accept in his own church. Ambrose had John 13.4–11 read out as he did the washing (or just before it):

Jesus rose from the meal, took off his outer garment, picked up a towel, and girt himself with it. Then he poured water into a basin and began to wash his followers' feet and wipe them with the towel he was girt with.

Then he came to Peter, who said to him, "Do you, Lord, wash my feet?" Jesus in answer said to him, "You do not grasp what I am doing, but you will know afterward."

Peter said, "At no time will you wash my feet." Jesus replied, "If I do not wash you, you will not be on my side."

Simon Peter said: "Lord, not my feet only, but my hands and head as well." Jesus told him: "The person who has bathed needs no further washing. You men are clean— well, not all." For he knew his betrayer—that is why he said not all were clean.

The Gospel of John goes on to say that this is an example of humility, which the disciples should practice with each other. Ambrose admits that this is one lesson from the reading, but that there is a deeper meaning, too. Judas has just left the table at this point in the Gospel, driven along by the devil (John 13.2), and Ambrose thinks Jesus is protecting the other men from the devil's power. He says that the feet merit special concern. When Jesus says that the bathed are clean, that refers to baptism:

> In baptism every fault is wiped out. Fault, then, disappears; but when Adam was felled, a venom was released on his feet, so you wash the feet, to raise a special protection of the point where the devil subverted him. You wash the feet to wash away the serpent's venom. (S 3.7)
>
> Peter was clean, but his feet must be washed, since he had the sin inherited from the first man, at the time when the serpent felled him and misled him into error. Thus

Peter's feet were washed to remove the hereditary sin. Our personal sins are removed by baptism. (*M* 32)

The idea of a devil's bite seems particular to Ambrose. Josef Schmitz thought that Ambrose alone held to this legend (G 178–79). But Pier Franco Beatrice claims that Ambrose was drawing on a mélange of Middle Eastern glosses on Genesis 3.15, where the Lord says to the serpent (in the Latin Ambrose read), "I will place hostility between you and the woman, between your seed and hers. He will crush your head, and you will scheme against his feet."[7] But it is quite a stretch to say that mankind was crippled ever after by a serpent sting to the feet, and that baptismal foot washing eliminates that legacy.

That is why Augustine did not accept Ambrose's explanation in his own baptisms—though, as we shall see, he used the idea to counter Pelagian denials of original sin. He, like Ambrose, departed from Roman practice in washing baptizands' feet— but only as a sign of humility. He thought it was wrong to say that baptism itself did not cleanse away all sin. But, of course, Ambrose thought washing the feet was an integral part of baptism, an action that went all the way from the renunciation of the devil through to the final "seal" (*signum*) before the neophytes left the baptistry (G 170–73). The reason for this difference between Ambrose and Augustine lies, apparently, in different conceptions of original sin. Ambrose distinguished between personal sin and hereditary guilt. He thought the first category the more serious one, which is why he equated it with Peter's threefold renunciation of Christ. Those most serious sins were removed by the total immersion; the inherited tendency to sin was washed away by the bishop's washing of the feet.

Augustine, by contrast, thought of original sin as pervading the whole of a person's life, affecting all personal sins, and even preexisting personal responsibility—a point he illustrated by pointing to the selfish actions of newborn infants (C 1.8, 11). We cannot know what Augustine was thinking as Ambrose washed his feet in 387, but he must have considered carefully what Ambrose professed by the time he departed from his teaching on this point.

After the washing of their feet, the neophytes received a "spiritual seal"—*spiritale signaculum*.

> After the font, there is still something to be completed, when the Holy Spirit is infused by the bishop's prayer, "the spirit of wisdom and understanding, the spirit of counsel and strength, the spirit of knowledge and reverence, the spirit of fearing God" [Isaiah 11.2], in short, the seven virtues of the Spirit. In fact, all virtues are those of the Spirit, but these are, as it were, cardinal, in the sense of outstanding. What is so outstanding as reverence? What so outstanding as knowledge of God? What so outstanding as strength? What so outstanding as the counsel of God? What so outstanding as the fear of God? Just as fear of the world is weakness, so is fear of God a great power. These are the seven virtues of your sealing—"the manifold wisdom of our God" [Ephesians 3.10], as the Apostle says. (S 3.8–10)

The special emphasis on the Spirit in this last part of the baptism reflects Ambrose's insistence that the whole action is suffused with the power of the Trinity.

> You have understood most deeply because you were baptized in the name of the Trinity. Everything we did here was subject to the divine working [*mysterium*] of the Trinity. At every point Father, Son, and Holy Spirit were one

action, one holiness, despite their appearance in different roles. How is this? It was God who anointed you, the Lord who signed you, and the Holy Spirit who lodged in your heart. Recognize another thing, that just as the Holy Spirit is in your heart, so Christ is in your heart. In what way? You find in the Song of Songs [8.6] Christ saying to his church, "Place me as a seal on your heart, as a seal on your arms." That is how God anointed you, and Christ signed you.

In what way? Because you were signed with the shape of the cross, and therefore of his passion. You received a seal that gave you his likeness, so you could rise in his image, his own image that was crucified and "lives in God" [Romans 6.10]. Your old man, submerged in the font, was crucified and rose up to God.

Further, you have this singularity, that while God called you, and you were singularly crucified with Christ, there is also the singular gift of the spiritual seal; you see singular persons in the Trinity but see their unity in the divine secret [mysterium].

And what did the Apostle say to you, in the reading two days ago? "There are differences in favors, though all are from one Spirit, differences in services but from one Lord, differences in activity but one Lord activating them all" [1 Corinthians 12.4–6]. In everything, he says, God is the agent. And it is written of the Spirit of God: "One and the same Spirit distributes favors as he will" [1 Corinthians 12.11]. So the Spirit distributes favors to you as he wills, not as he is ordered, especially since the Spirit of God is the Spirit of Christ. Hold to this, that the Holy Spirit is the Spirit of God, the Spirit of Christ, the Spirit-Champion [paraclete]. (S 6.5–9)

Ambrose is so intent on showing the Trinity at work throughout the whole baptismal process that he does not bother to say what physical act conveyed a bestowal of the spiritual seal. He refers to unction and to the sign of the cross, but they had been used already in the process. Something distinctive must have been done for the *spiritale signaculum*. Perhaps it was a breathing on the person (*sufflatio*) or a laying on of hands (as happened in other places). Later Christians tried to see in this "sealing" the beginnings of the separate sacrament of confirmation and looked for appropriate acts connected with that. But we have seen that Ambrose thinks of the whole sequence of actions in the baptistry as one baptism. That applied to the next act as well, the clothing in white.

The neophytes must have resumed their regular garments when they left the pool. But over them now were draped ceremonial vestments of white, probably of linen (G 22–23), which had special meaning for Ambrose. He relives the moment when the neophytes led the procession into the Basilica Nova. These newly initiated Christians must have felt very special indeed as they were anointed by the Father, clothed in Christ, and rinsed by the Spirit and showered with his gifts.

As you entered [the Basilica Nova] angels were gazing. They saw the human condition, one that was beforehand tainted with the squalor of sin, now suddenly refulgent. They asked, "What is this cohort coming up from the desert all in white?" [Song of Songs 8.5]. Even the angels were stunned. Would you understand their wonder? Listen as Peter explains that what is given us "the angels long to see" [1 Peter 1.12]. Or, again, "What eye has not seen, ear has not heard, God has prepared for those loving him" [1 Corinthians 2.9]. So ponder what you have received. The holy prophet David saw this favor in a foreshadowing and longed for it. Would you know what he longed for? Then hear again, "You will sprinkle me with hyssop and I shall be cleansed; you will wash me and I shall be whiter than snow" [Psalms 51.7]. Why whiter? Because snow, however white, is quickly blackened with dirt and spoiled, while the favor you have received, if you hold to what you receive, will be lasting and eternal. (S 2.5–6)

The neophytes are clothed in Christ, as Paul said in the passage Augustine read in the garden.

> You have received these white vestments to show that, having put off the wrappings of sin, you have clothed yourselves in the chaste covering of innocence. . . . For the baptized appears cleansed both under the Law and under the Gospel. Under the Law because Moses with a branch of hyssop sprinkled the blood of the lamb [Exodus 12.21–22; this reemphasizes Ambrose's teaching that the neophytes had been baptized in *blood* and water], and under the Gospel because Christ's vestments were "white as snow" when he showed [at the Transfiguration, Matthew 17.2] the glory of his Resurrection. He is whiter than snow whose sins are forgiven. That is why the Lord says through Isaiah, "If your sins are like scarlet, I shall make them white as snow" [Isaiah 1.18]. (M 34)

They are not only the image of Christ but of the church, which is reborn in them:

> The church, having put on these vestments through "the bath of rebirth" [Titus 3.5] says in the Song of Songs [1.4], "I am black and lovely, O you daughters of Jerusalem"— black through the fragility of the human condition, lovely through favor, black because made up of sinners, lovely

because of the sacredness of faith. Seeing these vestments, the stunned daughters of Jerusalem say, "What cohort comes up all in white?" [Song of Songs 8.5]. She was black, so how is she suddenly white?

Even the angels were puzzled when Christ ascended; the heavenly powers were puzzled that flesh could enter heaven. They asked, "Who is this king of glory?" When some were saying, "Lift the gates, principalities, and let the eternal gates be lifted up, so the king of glory can enter," others were puzzled and asked, "Who is this king of glory?" [Psalms 24.7–8]. In Isaiah, too, you find the powers of the heavens puzzled and saying, "Who is this who comes up from Edom, with red clothes from Bozrah, but beautiful in a white cloak?" [Isaiah 63.1].

When Christ sees his church in white vestments— he who for the church had put on ragged clothes, as you find in the book of Zachariah [3.3]—or he sees the soul clean and rinsed by the bath of rebirth, he says, "Lo, you are beautiful, my near one, lo you are beautiful, your eyes like a dove's" [Song of Songs 4.1]—like the dove in whose likeness the Holy Spirit descended from heaven [Luke 3.22].

Later it is said: "Your teeth are like a flock of shorn goats rising from the waters, which all bear twins and suffer no sterility. Your lips are like dyed cloth" [Song of Songs 4.2–3]. No slight tribute, this, primarily by the winning comparison to goats—for we know they safely graze in steep places and find food on the heights without danger. And when shorn, they are not weighed down—the church is like them, since it has the many virtues of souls that have shed their sins in the water [of baptism], who offer to Christ their belief in the mysteries and their moral favor, both speaking of the cross of the Lord Jesus.

In all this the church is beautiful; so God says to her, "You are all in beauty, my near one, there is nothing to blame in you" [Song of Songs 4.7] because your sins were submerged. "Come here out of Lebanon, my spouse, come out of Lebanon, you shall arrive, shall transcend all by the impulse of belief" [Song of Songs 4.8]. For the church, in renouncing the world, has transcended creation to reach Christ. (*M* 35–39)

This paean to whiteness is an effective counterblast to Melville's later hymn to an evil whiteness in *Moby-Dick*. Melville describes white at the core of a bleak universe, the sinister white light of a deceiving innocence. Ambrose celebrates a rain-rinsed translucence of the heavens. That is the reality—the heart of brilliance, not the heart of darkness—into which the neophytes were led from the font.

In their stunning white garments the newly baptized were ready to join the larger community in its procession out from the Basilica Vetus to the Basilica Nova. Given the processional culture described by Peter Brown, this probably took a long and circuitous route. An indication that the neophytes in their shining garments led the procession is given by the way Ambrose quotes the Song of Songs: "What cohort comes up from the desert dressed in white?" (*S* 4.5). Ambrose gives Psalm 23 a baptismal reading in his talks to the neophytes, and Satterlee suggests that they or the community sang it together or antiphonally during the procession.[8]

The Lord nourishes me, and nothing shall I lack. He shelters me in a pasture area. He has led me to water that restores me. He has turned my life around. He has brought me along the path of right, for his honor's sake. Should I walk in the very shadow of death, I fear no evil, since you are with me. Your rod and your staff are my assurance—the rod is rule, and the staff is punishment, which refer to the eternal power of Christ and to his bodily suffering: the first made us, the second redeems us. You spread in my sight a table protected from those who trouble me. You honor my head with oil, and an inebriating cup that is a wonder. (*S* 5.3.13)

This would be part of the music at his baptism that Augustine shed tears over (*C* 9.14).

When the neophytes went to the front of the basilica, Ambrose told them: "You are able to approach the altar. Because you have approached, you are able to see what you have not seen" (*S* 3.11)—so there was a screen between the nave (where they had been before during the mass of the catechumens) and the chancel area. Gathered there, they heard for the first time the Lord's Prayer, something guarded like the creed by the secrecy code (*disciplina arcana*). Ambrose would not expound the prayer until the following Friday (*S* 5.18–30). By then, the neophytes would finally know the full meaning of what they had experienced.

AFTER THE FONT

T he newly baptized would probably have some kind of Easter feast to break their long Lenten fast. Augustine would be welcomed into the Christian community by his African mother, brother, cousins, students, and friends. Some Milanese friends, like Mallius Theodore, no doubt shared the festivity. Perhaps his priest friend Simplician had his own Easter duties to attend to with his flock. The new Christians were not yet fully integrated into the church community—but only because they were set apart to be honored. They were freshly won prizes of the faith. Wearing their white garments all week long, they had a special place in the basilica when they attended Mass. Then they withdrew to their own quarters, probably the baptistry now, where Ambrose could help them relive what they had done, revealing layer on layer of mystical meaning in the act, pointing to the water, to the cross, to images of the dove.

We have two written accounts of what Ambrose said to the neophytes in his week-long discourses after their baptism—*De Sacramentis* and *De Mysteriis* for his week of talks after baptism.[1]

I have referred to them throughout the preceding chapters describing the baptismal rite. But Ambrose did not reveal the full meaning of what neophytes had undergone until they were securely in the sacred community, no longer excluded by the *disciplina arcani*. That is why the exposition of the Lord's Prayer came only in this week following their initiation. *De Sacramentis* is a record, in very simple language, taken down by a scribe with no concern for the attention of outsiders. *De Mysteriis* is a deeper reflection, written carefully, but with some regard for the *disciplina arcani* in case outsiders read it.

Though each was probably put in its present form later than 387, they reflect a long-settled view of the ritual that Ambrose presided over for many years, twelve of them before Augustine's baptism. The texts reflect the fact that Ambrose was teaching the neophytes at the same time that he was observing the ordinary readings of the Mass for the octave of Easter (*S* 2.2.3, 2.7.23, 3.2.8, 6.2.9 and *M* 22, 31). Suzanne Poque has traced the way Augustine imitated Ambrose in this respect, preaching his special Easter instructions after the sermons *de tempore*.[2] She suggests that the neophytes' instruction took place after the regular Mass, perhaps at night

The most striking aspect of *De Sacramentis* and *De Mysteriis* is the extensive array of typological prophecies applied to the salvation won in baptism. I list them separately below, and they come to fourteen. So, day by day, this is the way Ambrose impressed on neophytes the immensity of what had happened to them in the font.

DE SACRAMENTIS

Monday

In this first post-Easter talk, Ambrose goes over again the significance of the Effetha (2–3), the prebaptismal anointing (4), the renunciation of the devil (5–6), and the blessing of the water (15). Then he begins a listing of the prefigurations (types) of baptism, asserting that the Christian mysteries are older than the Jewish ones, since some of the signs (the Red Sea, the Flood) preceded Moses being given the Law (12, 23). The types are:

1. PASSAGE THROUGH THE RED SEA "Whoever passes through this font goes from earthly things to heavenly things—for it is a passing over, a Pasch, it is the Passover passing from sin to life, from guilt to grace, from taintedness to holiness—who goes through this font dies not but rises" (12). Paul said the passage through the sea was done "in foretype" (*figura*). Ambrose adds: "What was foretype for them is fact for us" (20).

2. THE CURE OF NAAMAN (2 KINGS 5.1–14) When Naaman sought a cure for his leprosy, Elisha told him to go wash seven times in the river Jordan. Naaman asked why he could not bathe in his own land's rivers, but Elisha said Jordan was more potent. Ambrose says: "It is not just any water that heals, only that heals that has been favored by Christ. The substance is one thing, the operative principle is another. Water has its operation, but the effect comes from the Holy Spirit" (15). The same is true of the blessed water in the font when the Spirit descends on it.

3. THE BAPTISM OF JESUS When Jesus was baptized the Spirit descended on him "in semblance like a dove." Then the Father spoke from heaven, so the entire Trinity is in the act of baptizing (16–18).

4. NOAH'S FLOOD "The Flood, too, was already a foretype of baptism" (23). Ambrose broke off here because his voice was giving out—and no wonder, with all the preaching before, during, and after Easter. His biographer said that when Ambrose died, it took five bishops to do what he had done alone at times like this (P 38).

Ambrose resumes by finishing the tale of the Flood. Noah and family survived the water, but the corrupt people died. So there is washing that works and washing that does not. The pagan baths clean the body but not the soul. Jewish baths are either beside the point or significant only as foretypes. And the foretypes are fulfilled "in us, for whom their truth is revealed" (2).

5. THE POOL OF BETHESDA (JOHN 5.1–12) When an angel disturbed the pool's water, the first one into it was cured of whatever illness he had. When a man could not get into the pool, Jesus cured him by a word, since it is his cross that gives force to baptism (3–7). Still, the pool is also a type because the angel blesses by disturbing it (8–9), as Ambrose had disturbed the font by dipping the cross in it. Though only one was cured after each disturbance of the water at Bethesda, all who go into the baptismal font are saved.

6. ELISHA'S AXHEAD (2 KINGS 6.1–7) As Elisha leads a party seeking new land, one of his company loses the head of his ax in the Jordan. He is distressed, because the ax was borrowed.

> When the head flew off the ax of Elisha's son as he chopped down a tree, it fell into the Jordan. But at Elisha's prayer it floated up. This is another type of baptism. Why? Because the unbaptized man is like iron weighed down and submerged. But when he has been baptized, he is iron no longer but is buoyant by nature like the wood of a fruit tree. And here is another foretype. The ax was being used to cut down wood. The head flew from the ax and, being iron, sank. Elisha's son did not know what to do; this alone he knew, to turn to the prophet and ask for help. Then he

threw the ax shaft in and the iron floated up. You see in this
that all human weakness is raised up by the cross. (11)

7. MOSES AND SWEET WATER (EXODUS 15.23–25) When
those wandering in the wilderness could not drink the waters of
Marah because of their bitterness, Moses cast a branch into it
and it sweetened the water. So does the cross make life's bitter-
nesses sweet—a reference to the crucifix being dipped into the
font (12–13). Here Ambrose speaks of original sin, of the Fall of
Man, of the curse of death: "You are earth, and to earth you shall
go down" (Genesis 3.14). But burial at the font is not in earth but
in sweet water, from which life arises, not death (16–19).
Ambrose reminds the neophytes of their threefold profession in
the font and their anointing afterward (20–24).

Wednesday

Ambrose has his audience relive their anointing, and the washing
of their feet.

8. THE WATERS OF GENESIS On the fifth day of creation, God
made the waters "bring forth living creatures" (Genesis 1.20). So
the waters of baptism will let the baptized swim through storms
like the living fish of Genesis 3. Ambrose explains the washing of
the feet with reference to the devil's bite on Adam's foot (4–7).
Then the "seal" is explained (8–10).

9. THE BLIND MAN AT THE POOL OF SILOAM Jesus cured the
blind man by putting clay on his eyes and telling him to wash it
off in the pool (John 9.6–11). This is what Ambrose was referring to at Epiphany when he said that the competentes had mud
put on their eyes, which would be removed by the waters of the
font (11–12).

Thursday

Ambrose explains that they entered the baptistry on Easter just as the high priest entered the inner Temple only once a year.

10. THE ROD OF AARON In the inner Temple was kept the rod of Aaron, which had withered and then come back to life—so the neophytes were dried and lifeless until revivified like "a plant by the rivers of water" (Psalms 1.3). The neophytes share the priestly status of Aaron (1 Peter 2.9). They are like the sweet savor of the Temple (2–4).

The rest of this discourse is on the Eucharist. Melchizedek was a type of Christ in offering bread and wine, and this shows that Christian foretypes antedate the Jewish rites, since Melchizedek lived before the Law was given (10–12). The bread and wine are truly changed into the body and blood of Christ (13–28).

Friday

Continuing the discussion of the Eucharist, Ambrose notes that the priest mixes water and wine in the Communion chalice. A type of this is:

11. MOSES STRIKING WATER FROM THE ROCK (EXODUS 17.5–7) When his followers are about to stone Moses because he led them into a desert where there is no water, the Lord orders him to go forward to a rock and then to strike it with his staff, and water pours out.

> When the bishop touches the chalice, water streams in the chalice—it is a spring of eternal life, and the people of God drink, all those who have pursued God's grace.

This might seem less a type of baptism than of the Eucharist. But it is linked with the cleansing of the soul by the image that immediately follows:

12. WATER AND BLOOD FROM CHRIST'S SIDE (JOHN 19.34)

When a soldier stabbed a lance into Christ's side, it released water and blood (John 19.34)—as the neophytes were baptized in water and blood: "Water to cleanse, blood to redeem" (4).

Now Ambrose uses a close reading of the Song of Songs to indicate the union of the believer with Christ in the Eucharist (5–17). This is followed by an analysis of the Lord's Prayer (18–30). On the meaning of "give us this day our *epiousion* bread" (Matthew 6.11, Luke 11.3), he notes that the Greek adjective *epiousios* comes from the prefix *epi* (over, for, after) plus *ousia* (being). The word is so rare that other usage does not give a guide to what it means. There are several possibilities:

+ "Above-being" bread could mean surpassing all being—Jerome translates it *supersubstantialis* in Matthew. That is one sense Ambrose gives it here, applying it to the Eucharist (24).
+ "For-being bread" could mean necessary to our being, what we require daily—Jerome translates it *quotidianus* in Luke. Ambrose accepts this as a second meaning, but still applying it to the Eucharist—he says his neophytes should take communion daily (25).
+ "After-being bread" could mean a future bread—either as tomorrow's bread (*crastinus*) or as the bread at the banquet of the End Time. This latter meaning, in accord with the eschatological nature of the Lord's Prayer, is favored by modern scholars.

Augustine does not wrestle with this difficult word when he explains the Lord's Prayer to his own baptizands (though he will do it before immersion, not after it).

Saturday

In his brief final address, Ambrose stresses again the Nicene doctrine of the Trinity, saying that they have been anointed by the Father, signed by the Son, and sealed by the Spirit in their baptism (1–10). Then he admonishes them to pray "in secret" (Matthew 6.6)—that is, with a private serenity and confidence, and observing the decorum which forbids women from speaking out in church (11–26).

DE MYSTERIIS

In this other account of the Easter octave instruction, Ambrose has his neophytes relive their sensations as they first saw the "holy of holies" and experienced its ritual. He mentions more of the types that foreshadowed baptism. Some of these are the same as the ones mentioned in *De Sacramentis*, but some are different.

13. THE SPIRIT MOVING OVER THE WATERS (GENESIS 1.2) Ambrose invoked the Spirit to descend upon the font and make the waters shape a new Christian identity in the baptizands, as the Spirit moved over the waters in the act of creation (9).

14. THE RAVEN AND THE DOVE (GENESIS 8.7–8) Ambrose mentioned Noah's Flood as a type of baptism in *De Sacramentis* but not the fact that Noah released a raven, which did not return, and a dove that did. He says these are types of the sin renounced at the font and the Spirit that brought peace (10).

Throughout *De Mysteriis*, Ambrose repeatedly emphasizes what the baptizands *saw* in the baptistry (6. 8, 10). This stress on the visual makes it likely that they were back in the baptistry for this instruction. He switches to the present tense: "You see the water, you see the wood, you are looking at the dove. Can you doubt the divine thing?" (10). The water was before them. So was the crucifix that was dipped in the water. Where was the dove, that they could look on it (*aspicis*)? Most likely it was depicted in fresco or mosaic, engaged in one of the dove's actions that Ambrose described (moving over water, returning to the ark, descending on Jesus):

> The water is that in which the body is plunged, so all fleshly sin can be washed away—for all offense is buried there. The wood is that to which the Lord Jesus was nailed when he suffered for us. The dove is the shape in which the Holy Spirit came down, as you have learned from the New Testament, the one who breathes peace into your soul and serenity into your mind. (11)

Ambrose runs through some of the same types mentioned in *De Sacramentis*—the passage of the Red Sea, the bitter water of Marah, the healing of Naaman (12–18). Then he expounds 1 John 5.6–8: "The one who arrives through water and blood is Jesus Messiah—not in water alone, but in water and blood. The Spirit gives witness to this, since the Spirit is truth. Thus there are three witnesses, the Spirit and water and blood, and the three are one." Ambrose applies this passage to baptism:

> I see everyday water. Does it have the power to cleanse, after I have often plunged into it without its cleansing me? Recognize that water without the Spirit cannot cleanse. That is why you have read that the three witnesses are one in baptism, water and blood and Spirit, since if one is taken away there is no sacredness in baptism. For what is water without the cross of Christ? A common substance with no sacred power. Yet without water there is no divine effect of rebirth, for "unless a man be reborn of water and the Spirit, he cannot enter the realm of heaven" [John 2.5]. Even a

catechumen believes in the cross of Christ; but unless he is baptized in the name of the Father, and of the Son, and of the Holy Spirit, he cannot have his sins forgiven or drink of spiritual favor. Accept, then, that this water does not lack effect. [At the pool of Siloam] one person was cured, but now all are—or, rather, one is: the whole Christian people. For some, there is only "false water" [Jeremiah 15.18]. The baptism of unbelievers does not heal, it does not cleanse, it pollutes. The Jew immerses pots and pans, as if inanimate things could have guilt or favor. (19–23)

In another passage that seems to refer to a depiction of a dove in the baptistry, Ambrose hears an objection (as in a diatribe):

You may say, "That was a real dove sent down [over Jesus at baptism]; here there is the Spirit *as if* in dove form. How then can we say that there was the likeness and here is the reality?" Yet the Greek scripture says that the Spirit descended in appearance [*species*] like a dove. What is more real than the divinity which is unchanging? No creature can be true reality, but only an appearance which can evanesce or change. Nonetheless the innocence of the baptized is real, not apparent—as the Lord says, "Be wise as serpents, innocent as doves" [Matthew 10.16]. Rightly then does the appearance of a dove descend here to remind us to be innocent as the dove. (25)

Finally, in this place as in *De Sacramentis*, Ambrose explains the anointing after baptism, the washing of the feet, the white garments, the seal, and the Eucharist as Christ's real presence (26–54). He ends by repeating that the union of the saved with the Lord in the Eucharist is figured forth in the Song of Songs (55–59). It is appropriate that Ambrose should conclude on a mystical note, using a favorite text, the Song of Songs, to describe the soul's ascent to God. Craig Alan Satterlee describes his whole preaching technique as "mystagogical."[3] He introduces his hearers into a secret knowledge system that is entirely activated by the love of God. The dynamism of the Trinity, as he expounded it, is not a set of dry theological disputes of the sort Edward Gibbon made fun of. Each believer is introduced into the inmost council of the universe. In him or her the Spirit is praying through Jesus to the Father. There is no more intimate entry into the cosmic system than the relation of each believer to the Trinity. That is what baptism accomplished in the eyes of Ambrose, and in the eyes of his attentive audience—none more attentive than Augustine, as he would demonstrate in a long life of pondering what he had been introduced to at Milan in the Lent and Easter season of 387.

PART III

HIPPO

9

———

BAPTISM IN AFRICA

For a variety of reasons having to do with his African duties, Augustine's approach to baptism differed at a basic level from Ambrose's. Ambrose had a mystical, poetic, and all-inclusive theology of Christian initiation. He saw baptism as the culmination of the entire sacred history leading up to Jesus's fulfillment of all the prophecies that pointed directly to baptism. The whole meaning of the Trinity was enacted and revealed in the action at the font, which brought new Christians into the inner dialogue of the persons with each other in the Godhead. The reality of the church was embodied in the rebirth of humanity out of the saving waters.

Augustine, by contrast, had what has been called a "minimalistic" view of baptism, legalistic, almost mechanical, with further steps often needed to reach the full Christian life, beginning with the relatively impoverished procedures of infant baptism (in contrast to the rich indoctrination of Ambrose during Lent and the Easter octave).[1] Peter Brown sums up Augustine's sermons on baptism this way:

He will point out, with considerable courtesy to his audience, that the baptism of an adult did not necessarily mean a new start to his life; that the convert should think of himself, not as a healed man, but like the man found wounded on the road from Jerusalem to Jericho—saved from certain death by the ointment of baptism, he must, nevertheless, be resigned to spending a lifetime of precarious convalescence in the Inn of the Catholic Church. (B 203)

Why did Augustine depart so sharply from the sacramental maximalism of Ambrose on the issue of baptism? It was because his defense of baptism was formed in opposition to two heresies that Ambrose did not confront—Donatism and Pelagianism—which had their own forms of baptismal maximalism. Both these heresies demanded a high degree of purity in the ministers and recipients of baptism. Augustine would argue against both views that valid baptism is the effect of the act performed (*ex opere operato*), not of the actor performing it (*ex opere operantis*).

When Augustine returned to Africa in 388, he spent three years on his father's old estate at Tagaste, planning to live the retired scholar's life he idealized in Mallius Theodore. He gathered a like-minded group to live in celibate community. But in 391, when he went to Hippo to interview a potential recruit to that community, the people there dragooned him into the priesthood, just as had happened with Ambrose. The bishop of Hippo, Valerius, was a Greek speaker who wanted to use Augustine's Latin preaching skills. In 395, to keep Augustine from going elsewhere, Valerius had him consecrated as his fellow bishop (bishops could not leave their diocese once they were consecrated). This was, strictly speaking, against canon law, a point that would be urged against Augustine. But Valerius died within a year, leaving Augustine in full command of the see at Hippo.

He had to confront a situation for which his studies had not prepared him. The majority of Christians in Africa were Donatists, who considered Roman representatives along the continent's northern littoral foreign and heretical. The leading scholar of Donatism, W. H. C. Frend, says that "the Berber peoples of the Numidian high plains" were solidly Donatist, and "nothing like the dedicated sectarianism of rural Donatist Christianity in Numidia existed anywhere else in the Greco-Roman world."[2] But the Donatists were not confined to rural areas. There was a Donatist cathedral just down the street from Augustine's church in the port city Hippo, near enough for his congregation to hear the other worshipers at their service inside their own walls (*Epistulae* 29.11). Augustine had Donatists among his own relatives (*Epistulae* 52.4).

Donatism was born of the major persecution of Christianity (303–5) under the emperor Diocletian. The Traditores ("handersover"), so named because they escaped death by surrendering the Christian sacred texts, were despised by those who accepted martyrdom rather than collaborating with the persecutors. In the aftermath of the persecution, Traditores were denounced, as were those who were ordained as priests or consecrated as bishops by accused Traditores. The only way those who had deserted the faith could be reinstated was to start all over again, with a valid baptism by the uncontaminated. Those who did not submit to this rebaptism were forever excluded from the true church that followed the great bishop of Carthage, Donatus. This pure church celebrated its fidelity and that of the martyrs, whose shrines became power houses of the patriotic Africans who had defied an empire.

The situation of Augustine resembled somewhat that of Ambrose when Augustine observed him in Milan. Ambrose, too, succeeded a Greek-speaking bishop and faced an intransigent opposition that was in the majority when he took over—the Arian circle of his predecessor as bishop and the whole court apparatus of the emperor Valentinian. Ambrose, too, had to contain a threat from zealous martyr cultists. And the violence of the imperial soldiers in Milan was like that of the rural Circumcelliones ("enforcers") who carried their contempt for the Traditores into violence. One wonders if Augustine's dismissal of the tactics of Ambrose began to lessen as he faced his own ruling quandaries.

His first approach was to counter the majority status of the Donatists in Africa with a different majority—throughout the Western and Eastern Christian churches. Donatists were nationalists, who spoke to Africans in their native Berber language, one that Augustine never mastered. They rejected the Greek and Latin of the imperial courts. They saw the Traditores as cooperating with a foreign government. Augustine countered with the argument that the universal church was in the ecumenical councils, where Donatus was unknown. The Donatists relied on nationalism. Augustine reduced that to provincialism. How could the true church exist only in Africa, and only in one faction (*pars*) of African Christians?

> The Lord balanced the round earth so it would not wobble. How closely that resembles the building up of his church! Clouds thunder around the whole circuit of the globe, to herald the church's edification. Yet these frogs croak from their swamp: "There are no Christians but us."[3]

Writing to a member of the Rogatist faction of Donatists, one Vincent of Cartenna, Augustine mocks the idea that the whole world is full of an impure religion, whose integrity is confined to part of Africa:

> If anyone in any country of the world should be moved to repent his sins, he cannot find absolution till he looks for and finds Vincent of Cartenna, or his band of nine or ten, hiding in imperial Mauritania. . . . Shout as loud as you can

your claim that even if the gospel should be preached in Persia and India (as it has in fact long been preached there), no one there can be freed from his sins [by baptism] till he comes to Cartenna or its region. (*Epistulae* 93.21–22)

When Augustine argued that "Catholic" (from Greek *katholou*, through all) referred to the church throughout the world, Vincent proposed a different etymology, saying "Catholic" should mean "through all doctrines," which Donatists alone preserved in their entirety and integrity. Augustine answered drolly, "You fancy you are saying something clever. . . . With your permission, we do not accept that" (*Epistulae* 923.23).

Donatists argued that Traditores could not validly ordain or consecrate or baptize. Augustine answered that it is impossible to tell, one by one, who is a saint and who a sinner. Are we to grade baptism according to the virtue of its minister? That degrades the power of the sacrament, which is administered by Jesus through his body of believers, the church. When Donatists denounced the church as full of sinners and weak deserters, Augustine drew on the greatest thinker among the Donatists themselves, the African pioneer of scriptural hermeneutics, Tyconius. Though Tyconius had been excommunicated by the Donatists for not being rigorist enough, he considered himself a Donatist until his death ca. 390. Augustine at first felt reluctant to cite a schismatic on scriptural matters, but he admired the man's *Liber de Septem Regulis*, which established limits to the allegorical uses of the Bible, helping Augustine chasten the more extravagant typologies of Ambrose.

But one type that Augustine took from Tyconius was pivotal to much of Augustine's thought, especially in *The City of God*. The elder African thinker took the wheat and chaff of Matthew 3.12 and the net of mixed fish (some good, some bad) of Matthew 13.47–48 as types of the church. Here on earth, the church has both saints and sinners in it, not to be identified until the Final Judgment. Augustine used this to show that the Donatist ideal of a church made up only of saints is not the reality of life, where sinners can become saints and vice versa while living in the church. To popularize this view, and as propaganda against the Donatists, Augustine even wrote a long poem in accentual doggerel, parts of which run:

> Collect the wheat at world's loss,
> Winnowed then by Christ's cross. (174)
>
> . . . .
>
> To winnow only after reaping,
> Till then much falsehood we are weeping. (196–97)
>
> . . . .
>
> See church as net and world as sea,
> Where good and bad are mingled free.
> We sail on to the end of time,
> To see revealed what's yours, what's mine. (10–12)[4]

The earthly church is not the City of God, which is perfect only in heaven. We must live with many imperfections. Baptism in this world cannot be valid only when ministered by saints—otherwise it would be more valid if the minister were more saintly, and less so if he were a sinner. It is not the man who baptizes but Christ, acting in his mystical body, the church.

Augustine had one great obstacle to his position, the example of the African saint honored by both the Donatists and the imperial church. Saint Cyprian, bishop of Carthage, hid from the authorities during Diocletian's persecution of 250–51 but was executed during Valerian's persecution of 258. Between those dates he had a famous clash with Stephen, the bishop of Rome, over the validity of baptisms administered by heretics. Stephen thought them valid. Cyprian denied this. He thought heretics had to be rebaptized, since their first baptism was "not an ablution but a pollution" (*De Unitate Ecclesiae* 11). The Donatists defended their own rebaptizing of those baptized by Traditores by appealing to the venerated name of Cyprian. Augustine had to refute Cyprian while showing proper respect for the hero. This he did in his long work *De Baptismo*.

He is careful to refer to Cyprian as "the irenic bishop and splendid martyr." But he points out that even great and saintly men may err, as did Peter, "that first of apostles and most outstanding of martyrs," when Paul had to correct him on Jewish observances (Galatians 2.11–14).[5] Augustine admits that eighty African bishops agreed with Cyprian on rebaptizing heretics; but he points out that ecumenical councils rejected this practice (he does not rely on Stephen of Rome, since the pope was not considered infallible at the time). He commends Cyprian for the irenic tone he took, even as he erred. He quotes from the end of Cyprian's Letter 73:

> We write this, dear brother, with our modest capacity, not prescribing or prejudging, since each bishop should do what he thinks right, exercising his power of free will. We so far as possible do not argue about heretics with our associates and fellow bishops, with whom we maintain concord and the peace of the Lord.[6]

He points out that Cyprian, unlike the Donatists, kept in respectful touch with the whole church in the world (*Epistulae* 93.42).

Augustine's formalism (and formula-ism) is stated forthrightly: "Without hesitation I say that men can be baptized anywhere and by anyone, according to the form made sacred by the words of the Gospel, so they be sincere and act from faith."[7] The words of the Gospel that he is referring to are Christ's words at Matthew 28.19: "Going forth, then, teach all nations, baptizing them in the name of the Father and the Son and the Holy Spirit." As for the merits of a recipient of baptism, Augustine points out that emergency baptism of those in danger of death does not allow for a careful preparation and examination of intention—this is the kind of baptism he desired when he was ill (C 1.17) and the kind that was given his friend when that friend was unconscious (C 4.8).[8] On such grounds Augustine defended the practice of baptizing infants.[9] His legalism can be seen when he says that baptism by a heretic may be valid (*legitimus*) in itself but invalidly (*non legitime*) used outside the church.[10]

Augustine's view of baptism was constrained by attacks from another front—another form of sacramental maximalism, that of the Pelagians. It is sometimes thought that Pelagians denied the fall of man and thought of humans as perfect or perfectible. On the contrary, while they denied that original sin came from Adam, they did believe that individual sins of individual people were very real and reprehensible—and that made baptism, as wiping those sins out, all the more powerful and important (B 195–202). Popular myth sometimes presents Pelagians as libertines, though they were in fact ascetics, albeit of a refined and aristocratic sort. Peter Brown says of them: "The followers of Pelagius and Caelestius are the only religious group in Rome that will be condemned not only for being heretical, not only for being disturbers of the peace, but also for claiming to be superior to everybody else" (B 189). In dealing with Donatists, Augustine and his opponents both revered Saint Cyprian, so Augustine had to pry Cyprian very gently out of their grasp. With the Pelagians he found that both sides revered Ambrose, though somewhat diffidently in the case of the Pelagians, so he had to keep thrusting Ambrose into their resisting arms.

Of course the African Donatists were in Augustine's backyard (or down the street from him). The Pelagians were not. Brown finds them mainly in the wealthy families of Sicily and Rome. But Augustine found himself connected with them through two Paulinuses. Paulinus of Milan had come to Africa, and he helped organize the council in Carthage that condemned Pelagius's ally Caelestius when he arrived in Africa after the Visigoths took Rome in 410. This Paulinus is the one Augustine asked to write down his memories of Ambrose at the time when Augustine was citing Ambrose against the Pelagians. The other Paulinus, Paulinus of Nola, was an admirer of Augustine (he asked him to write a tribute to his friend and fellow African bishop Alypius). But he was also a friend of Pelagius and of Pelagius's supporter Julian of Eclanum. He wrote a poem dedicated to Julian on the occasion of his marriage (B 210–12). Peter Brown suspects that Augustine was slow to engage with Pelagians because they had such close ties with the influential Paulinus of Nola. When he did enter into prolonged debate with the Pelagians, Augustine had to assert his own orthodoxy on such subjects as original sin and infant baptism by aligning himself persistently with Ambrose and his practice of washing feet to cancel the effects of Adam's fall.

The differences in the approach of Ambrose and Augustine to baptism were conditioned by the different opposition each man faced. Ambrose fought on two fronts. He aroused popular resistance to the imperial court with his street people, but he fashioned sophisticated arguments for his Greek-speaking Arian foes. He was living in a cosmopolitan center where Trinitarian controversy was long entrenched. Augustine's immediate audience was less educated than Ambrose's, as we can see from the doggerel poem he felt he had to use to popularize his ideas. Populism was not on his side but arrayed against him in the Berber-speaking ranks of the Donatists. On the other hand, when fighting with the polished Julian, who knew Greek, Augustine had to draw on the Latin classics in a way that he had earlier given up doing, just to show he was not what Julian called him, "a donkey keeper" and "what passes for a philosopher with Africans" (U 4.56, 5.11).[11]

To see how Augustine's baptismal teaching differed from Ambrose's, consider their instruction of the competentes in the symbol. Ambrose discussed the various Trinitarian heresies rejected by the creed. Augustine, in a more down-to-earth pedagogy, explains the implications of the creed's first article this way:

I believe in God the Father almighty. See how quickly it is said, yet how powerful it is. He is God, he is Father—God in majesty, Father in kindness. Happy we, then, to find in our God our Father. Let us believe in him and hope all things for ourselves, since he is almighty. That is why we believe in *God the Father almighty.*

Let no one of you say, "He cannot forgive my sins."
Why not? He is almighty.
But you say, "I have sinned so much."
I repeat, he is almighty.
You say again, "I have committed such sins as I cannot be freed or cleansed from."
I answer, he is still almighty.

Recall what you sing to him in the psalm [103.1–3]: "Praise the Lord, my soul, and keep in mind all his kindnesses, who was forgiving of all your sins and heals all your illness." That is why we need for him to be almighty. (*Sermones* 213)

Augustine's pastoral care comes through a passage like that. God's almightiness can seem remote and intimidating, but when it is combined with fatherhood, it loses its harshness and becomes an invitation to intimacy. (Augustine, unlike Ambrose, had been a father himself, and a very loving one.) Almightiness ceases to stun or terrify when it is seen as the empowerment of fatherly love.

He continues the lesson:

Now I will tell you all the things he cannot do. He cannot die. He cannot sin. He cannot be deceived or make a mistake. All these things he cannot do; and if he could, he would not be almighty. . . . So believing him, profess the creed, and recite it back. Accept, then, what you are to retain in memory, and recite back, and never forget. (*Sermones* 213)

Looking forward to the time when the competentes have to recite the creed from memory, he is solicitous for those who might have trouble with the task. People were apparently less educated, in his provincial town, than in Ambrose's in the imperial center. There may have been some whose first language was Berber and who had trouble with the Latin of the creed. Whatever the reason, he tells them not to be upset if, at the beginning, they are not word-perfect. They will often hear the creed repeated, now that they are among the initiates.

Eight days from now you will recite what you learned today. Let your godparents, assisting you, begin teaching you so you will be prepared, showing you how to wake at dawn to say the assigned prayers. We began by giving you the symbol, so that you may carefully learn it by heart. But do not be flustered if in a panic you cannot recite. Do not worry—we are your fathers, we carry no sticks and whips like schoolmasters. If you fail at the words, do not fail at belief. (*Sermones* 213)

Augustine famously resented the beatings he received in his school at Madauros (C 1.23). One gets the feeling that if a member of Augustine's community came to him with personal troubles, he would be given a warmer welcome than Ambrose gave him. Though Augustine received from Ambrose a wonderful scriptural education in the Lent and Easter season of 387, it is no wonder that it took him decades to warm to Ambrose as a person.

THE RITUAL

I n the provincial town of Hippo Regius, Augustine had a much smaller arena for action than Ambrose had in his imperial capital.[1] Hippo was a harbor town on the northern coast of Africa (present Algeria). It disappeared after the Vandals attacked it while Augustine was dying, and was excavated by Erwan Marec, beginning in 1924.[2] It is estimated that Hippo had 30,000 to 40,000 inhabitants, as opposed to the 150,000 to 160,000 of Milan. Augustine's church was correspondingly small. Van der Meer wrote: "It is neither a very large nor a very striking building. Its measurements—60 by 126 (or, including the apse, 147) feet are those of the average fairly large main church in this area."[3] There were suburban churches, including one called Leontiana (*Sermones* 260), along with martyr shrines.

Augustine's baptistry was much smaller than Ambrose's. Its rectangular pool was only eight by six feet, as opposed to Ambrose's octagonal pool measuring twenty by twenty feet. The building enclosing the pool is so small—thirteen by fifteen feet—that, with Augustine and two presbyters inside, only one person had room for unclothing, immersion, and reclothing. That means that baptism had to be administered one at a time, and instruction before and after baptism took place in contiguous areas—a cate-chumeneum on one side and a consignatorium (sealing place) on the other.[4] This may be because in his town he had fewer appli-cants, or because he baptized in several churches. But it is likely that he did not want to concentrate baptisms in the Easter season, as was the custom. We know that he was against delaying baptism and that he favored infant baptism. He had asked for emergency baptism when he was sick as a child. He recognized that it was the custom to be baptized at Easter, but he thought that this was based on a misapprehension—that baptism was more valid on Easter, just as the Donatists said it was more valid if performed by a saintly man. He saw a connection between the heresy and the timing. He might, therefore, have welcomed the restricted room of the baptistry as an encouragement of early individual baptism. He said at the beginning of Lent:

> We shall be fasting along with the baptizands, antici-pating the day of their baptism, which occurs on Easter, and after that we end the fast for fifty days. There is no reason to place much emphasis on this, as if to baptize or to be baptized were not allowed except on the solemn Easter day. Any time in the year when baptism is needed or wanted it is valid, by the grant of the one who gave all the power to become the children of God [John 1.2], while we cannot celebrate the anniversary of the Lord's death on any but the one day of the year called Easter. So baptism must be clearly separated from Easter. One can be received on any day, while the other can be observed only on one. The first gives new life. The other recalls the memory on which our religion is based. Admittedly, most

of those seeking baptism prefer this day, but not because they are more saved then—they just want to join in the joy of the time. (*Sermones* 210.1)

Augustine's baptisms differed from Ambrose's, but it is difficult to say how much of this difference was intentional. The practices of Hippo may have been settled before Augustine took over. But the overarching difference seems to reflect a different attitude toward baptism on Augustine's part. The principal difference has to do with the order of instruction. The explanation of the "mysteries" (creed, exorcisms, renunciation of the devil, profession of belief, the anointings, the water, the crucifix, the dove, the baptism itself, the washing of feet, the anointing of the head, the seal of the Spirit, the Eucharist, the Lord's Prayer) is often referred to as mystagogy, and there were two basic approaches to the process. Some, like Ambrose, put the principal instruction after baptism, observing the *disciplina arcani*. Cyril of Jerusalem (ca. 313–86) agreed with this approach. He began the first of his instructions to the newly baptized this way: "Long have I yearned, you genuine and longed-for newborn of the church, to share with you the spiritual and heavenly mysteries.... Now let me speak outright what meaning the night of your baptism had for you."[5]

Others, like John Chrysostom and Theodore of Mopsuestia, felt that people should know beforehand what they were committing themselves to.[6] Augustine belonged to this latter school. Perhaps his predecessor Valerius, a Greek speaker, had already established Eastern practices. But it fit Augustine's sacramental minimalism and legalism to explain the process before people submitted themselves to it. Ambrose had a more mystical, even theatrical, approach, like that of the mystery religions that relied on "revelation"—as we can see from his frequent interjections of "Look!" and "See!" in his mystagogy. He liked the drama of a group undergoing long tutelage together. Augustine, dealing with individual baptisms, could not arrange the long and arduous indoctrination that Ambrose developed. Augustine's approach is less mystagogy than pedagogy. He explains the Lord's Prayer before baptism, not after. His explanations of the washing of the feet and of the Eucharist rely less on miracle and legend.

Augustine taught the competentes humility and repentance for sin during his Lenten sermons (*Sermones* 205–211A). He reminded them that the word *com-petentes* means "fellow applicants," just as *condocentes* were fellow teachers, *concurrentes* fellow athletes, and *considentes* fellow settlers (*Sermones* 216.1). They were to fast, wear sackcloth, and not bathe (they would be given a session at the baths on Holy Thursday—*Epistulae* 54.7, 10). When they underwent their *scrutamen*, they removed the sackcloth but stood on a goatskin (*cilicium*) as a renunciation of the goats who will be separated from the sheep in the last judgment (*Sermones* 216.11). As part of their exorcism, they had the devil banished by a hiss (*exsufflatio*, U 1.50).

Ambrose, it will be remembered, taught the creed on Palm Sunday. Augustine taught it a week earlier and had the competentes recite it back on Palm Sunday. He explained the term "symbol" as Ambrose had—it is a common pool of beliefs (*Sermones* 212.1). But he also used the other etymology as an authenticating instrument (like an indenture), saying it is a sign of identity (*Sermones* 213.2) or a password (*Sermones* 214.121). Whereas Ambrose taught the Lord's Prayer after baptism, Augustine expounded it on Palm Sunday (*Sermones* 56).

Augustine criticizes the common view that the petitions in the first part of the Lord's Prayer have to do with God and the later ones with his believers. After all, we cannot tell God what to do about himself. "Hallowed be thy name" does not make God more hallowed. "Thy kingdom come"—it will come, inevitably. "Thy will be done"—God will get his way, no matter what. Then what is the point of these first petitions? He says that the believers are asking that the name be hallowed *in and by us*—That the kingdom come *in us*, that we may be included in the coming kingdom; that his will be accepted *in us*, that we should not be guilty of resisting it. Thus all the opening prayers, like all the rest, concern the ones doing the praying, that they submit to God's power, which will prevail, either to our harm or our blessing. The petitions ask that it be for our blessing.

In the later petitions, Augustine does not, like Ambrose, deal with the Greek word *epiousion* applied to bread. He just accepts the Latin word *quotidianus*, and gives it three meanings: (1) our necessary physical nourishment, (2) the daily feeding on the Word of the Lord, which nourishes the soul, and (3) the Eucharistic bread (which Ambrose thought it principally meant, though he derived this meaning from *epiousion*, interpreting it as "the above-being bread"). For "forgive us our debts" (sins), Augustine argues against the Pelagian view of baptism, that it ends all sins. Augustine, with his baptismal minimalism, admits that some sins will continue to be committed even after baptism. He was fighting the practice of putting off baptism because all one's sins had to be committed before accepting it.

> Those ships that sail on after baptism will take on some leakage through human flaws—not necessarily enough to cause a shipwreck but enough to need bailing. Without such bailing the ship will gradually founder and eventually sink. This prayer is our way of bailing. (*Sermones* 56.11)
>
> Though all sins are forgiven in the bath of rebirth, we will end up on the shoals if we are not daily scrubbed by this holy prayer. . . . I am not talking about sins so mortal as to make one excommunicated . . . but, apart from these, other sins can be committed. (*Sermones* 56.12)[7]

On Easter eve, there was an all-night vigil with scriptural readings. Rather than the dazzling profusion of "types" that Ambrose used in his mystagogy, Augustine dwelt heavily on the symbol of the crossing of the Red Sea as a prophecy of baptism.[8]

> You are about to approach the holy font, where you will be rinsed in baptism, renewed in the saving bath of rebirth. You will be free of sin as you emerge from that bath. The past that haunted you will be obliterated there. Your sins will be like the Egyptians who chased the Israelites only so far as the Red Sea. Why only so far as the Red Sea? They can come only so far as the font made holy by the cross and the blood of Christ. Red Sea comes from red. Do you not see how something from Christ reddens the font? Use the eyes of faith. As you look on the cross, see the blood. As you see what hangs there, behold what pours down there. Christ's side was pieced by a lance and our ransom poured out. That is why baptism is signed with the cross, the water in which you are immersed as you cross the Red Sea. Your sins are your enemies, and they chase you only so far as the sea. When you enter the sea, you give them the slip. (*Sermones* 213.9)

It seems clear from passages like this that Augustine followed Ambrose's practice of dipping a crucifix into the font.

After the neophytes came out of the baptistry, one by one, Augustine bestowed the seal of the spirit. Ambrose did not indicate how he did this, but Augustine did it by the imposition of hands. Then the *infantes*, as he called them, returned to the church for their first reception of the Eucharist. It is probable that he explained the meaning of the Eucharist before their reception of it, since he did not want them to misunderstand what they were doing. He did not agree with Ambrose that the bread and wine were the literal body and blood of Christ. He ridiculed that idea. He notes that people turned away from Jesus when he said that he was the new manna, "the bread of life" (John 6.35–41). They took bread in a physical sense, not a spiritual one: "They thought Jesus was saying that they could cut him up, cook him like a lamb, and eat him" (*In Johannis Evangelium Tractatus* 11.5).

Augustine repeatedly says that Christ cannot be chewed, digested, and excreted. He says that Christ as bread refers to "the validity of the mystery (*virtus sacramenti*), not to the visibility of the mystery (*visibile sacramentum*), given to the one who eats inwardly, not outwardly, one who feeds his heart, not one who chews with his teeth" (*In Johannis Evangelium Tractatus* 26.12).

> What you see passes away, but what is invisibly symbolized does not pass away. It perdures. The visible is received, eaten, and digested [*consumitur*]. But can the body of Christ be digested? Can the church of Christ be digested? Can Christ's limbs be digested? Of course not. (*Sermones* 227)

For us to be united with Jesus we must be taken into him, not he into us. We must become his members (*In Johannis Evangelium Tractatus* 27.6).

> If you want to know what is the body of Christ, hear what the Apostle [Paul] tells believers: "You are Christ's body and his limbs [1 Corinthians 12.27]. If, then, you are Christ's body and his limbs, it is your symbol that lies on the Lord's altar—what you receive is a symbol of yourselves. When you say "Amen" to what you are, your saying it affirms it. You hear [the priest say], "The body of Christ," and you answer "Amen," and you must be the body of Christ to make that "amen" take effect. And why are you

bread? Hear again the apostle, speaking of this very symbol: "We are one bread, one body, many as we are" [1 Corinthians 10.17]. (*Sermones* 272)

Believers recognize the body of Christ when they take care to be the body of Christ. They should be the body of Christ if they want to draw life from the spirit of Christ. No life comes to the body of Christ but from the spirit of Christ. (*In Johannis Evangelium Tractatus* 26.13)

So insistent was Augustine that the body of Christ—the bread of Christ—was the whole body of believers that he explained to neophytes the whole process of their formation as a baking of Christ's bread in them:

This [Eucharistic] bread makes clear how you should love your union with one another. Could the bread have been made from one grain, or were many grains of wheat required? Yet before they cohered as bread, each grain was isolated. They were fused in water, after being ground together. Unless wheat is pounded, and then moistened with water, it can hardly take on the new identity we call bread. In the same way, you had to be ground by the ordeal of fasting and exorcism in preparation for baptism's water, and in this way you were watered in order to take on the new identity of bread..... But the dough does not become bread until it is baked in a fire. And what does fire represent for you? It is the [postbaptismal] anointing with oil. Oil, which feeds fire, is the mystery of the Holy Spirit.... The Holy Spirit comes to you, fire after water, and you are baked into the bread which is Christ's body. That is how your unity is symbolized. (*Sermones* 227)

So much was the bread a symbol of union that it was sent to other communities as a token of blessing.[9]

From this it appears that the postimmersion anointing (presumably of the head, as with Ambrose) was more important than the anteimmersion one, and was connected with the seal of the Spirit. Ambrose did not signal how he bestowed the seal, but Augustine did it with a laying on of hands.[10]

Augustine did not include a washing of the feet in the baptismal ceremony itself, lest it suggest some less inclusive forgiveness of sins—the way Ambrose made it the forgiveness of original sin, as opposed to actual sins. Since it was expected by custom, he separated it off during the octave of Easter, and he said it was just a sign of humility among the Christian brothers (*Epistulae* 55.33). Of the rite of baptism as complete in itself, he said:

> Approach the font forgiving your debtors, and you can be confident that all your sins are forgiven you, both the sin inherited from your parents because of Adams's first sin (it is because of this sin that you join with infants in embracing the favor of the Rescuer) and whatever sins you committed in your prior life. (*Sermones* 56.13)

The *infantes* put on the white linen outer garb that Augustine had worn himself in Milan. In Africa they also put on special sandals for the octave of Easter, not touching the earth in union with the risen Jesus (*Epistulae* 55.35).

Augustine gives a less complete picture of his baptism practices than Ambrose did, presumably because he encouraged and performed individual baptisms, for which the long and elaborate Lenten course would have been impractical and time-consuming if many of them occurred during the year. Since Augustine compared individual baptism to infant baptism and the emergency baptisms of the sick, his sacramental minimalism led to stripped-down ceremonies. Which is not to say that he understated the importance of baptism. His opposition to the Donatists and the Pelagians meant, among other things, that he had to defend his own emphases on baptism. He even ascribed miracles to the act of baptism. He criticized the superstition that water from the font could heal people, but he mounted a publicity campaign for baptism miracles, in opposition to the Donatist baptism stories.

A pious woman in Carthage who had breast cancer was instructed in a dream to go observe the neophytes coming away from baptism and ask the first woman she saw coming from the women's baptistry to bless the breast—and it was cured. When Augustine, on one of his preaching trips to Carthage, heard her story, he rebuked her for not making such an event better known.

In the same city, devils warned a man in dreams not to be baptized, but when he was, his gout disappeared. Another man who was paralyzed had been cured at his baptism, and Augustine and the Carthaginian bishop summoned him to testify to this.[11] Augustine was a sacramental minimalist in many ways, but he knew the popular means to encourage people to seek baptism, not only in the Easter season but whenever they meant to adopt the religion of Christ.

AUGUSTINE NEEDS AMBROSE

Ambrose and Augustine were men very different in temperament and repute, and their image for years reflected this difference. Ambrose was remembered and celebrated for his forcefulness, and Augustine for his inwardness. The iconography of Ambrose showed him as the scourge of heretics, the triumphant man entering Milan as a conqueror. That is how the city's gonfalon depicted him (fig. 1.1). There as elsewhere he towers over a recumbent (heretical) foe. On sculptures for the tomb of one of Milan's Visconti rulers, a central Ambrose hands off to the right a standard to an emperor and to the left a staff to a prosperous merchant, while on either side are allegorical representations of the ten cities subject to Milan.

The painter Bernardo Zenale (1511) shows Ambrose kneeling to the right of the Virgin while the baby Jesus hands over to him an episcopal crosier—and under his knees is a Roman soldier signifying the empire he crushed (fig. 11.1). Bramantino (1510) painted him kneeling over the foreshortened nude corpse of the heretic Arius. As late as 1941 Ambrose was still being shown

Figure 11.1 Bernardo Zenale, *Madonna and Child with Saints*, 1511.
Denver Art Museum collection: Gift of the Samuel H. Kress Foundation,
1961.173. Photography provided by the Denver Art Museum.

with his scourge on the Arengario Palace at the Piazza del Duomo in a sculpture by Arturo Martini. He tramples Roman soldiers under his horse while entering Milan.

Augustine, by contrast, is not shown as coercing others. His iconography is of inwardness and study. Two favorite images are of him among his books receiving a vision of Saint Jerome at his death and of his pacing beside a vast sea as the infant Christ tells him the Trinity is too vast to be understood. The best known of the former type are probably Botticelli's (1480) in Florence and Carpaccio's (1502) in Venice (fig. 11.2). Two examples of the second type are Botticelli's (1487) at the Uffizi and Pinturicchio's (1523) in Perugia (fig. 11.3).

Not surprisingly, given their different personalities, Augustine and Ambrose did not correspond with each other after Augustine returned to Africa. For years Augustine did not quote or cite Ambrose. Of course he was indebted to him for the first introduction of typology in the Jewish scripture, but he could have derived that from other sources after he left Milan. Nonetheless, in time he had to refer to Ambrose to credential himself after some began to question the sincerity of his conversion from Manicheism or the validity of his consecration as bishop during the lifetime of Valerius. Furthermore, as a bishop himself he came to need and use some of Ambrose's methods. He reluctantly adopted some coercive tactics, and he developed the cult of miracles he had formerly disdained. Most important, he recruited Ambrose in his knock-down, drag-out campaign against the Pelagians. On the point of legal coercion, Augustine found himself caught up in the violent conflict with Donatists. Both sides had used coercion in the past—foes of the Donatists when the emperor Constans sent Count Macarius to put them down in the 340s, and foes of the Catholics when the Berber chieftain Gildo sided with the Donatists in the 390s. The Donatists had also used the law against their own heretical faction of Maximianists. Peter Brown notes that Augustine had stood

Figure 11.2 Sandro Botticelli, *Saint Augustine*. Photo: Scala/Art Resource, NY.

Figure 11.3 Sandro Botticelli, *San Barnaba Altarpiece*. Panel of the Predella with the Vision of Saint Augustine Meditating on the Trinity. Photo: Scala/ Ministero per i Beni e le Attività culturali/Art Resource, NY.

apart from this struggle in his early African days, since he was a Manichean then, with no stake on either side, and for the first years of his return to Africa he concentrated on distinguishing himself from the Manichean body he had belonged to (B 272).

With the Manicheans he relied on challenges to public debate, and he hoped in later clashes with Donatists to pursue the same strategy. He tried to reduce the hostility on both sides, writing letters to Donatist bishops:

> Let us take out of play the unproductive charges that people on both sides hurl at each other. If you do not bring up the Macarian period, I pass over the circumcellions [roving Donatist bands]. Say that the latter have nothing to do with you, nor the former with me. The Lord's threshing floor is not yet winnowed, there is bound to be chaff among us both—let us pray only, and take steps, that together we may be his wheat. (*Epistulae* 25.6)

I ask you, what sense do these old quarrels make for us? The profound resentment of unbending partisans has kept the wounds of our congregations open for far too long, wounds whose deadened flesh has become insensate, so we feel no need for the doctor. (*Epistulae* 33.5)

He proposed public discussions, like those he had held with the Manicheans. If Donatists distrusted him, they could choose a Catholic spokesman more to their liking (*Epistulae* 34.5–6). But the Donatists did not like the way those debates had turned out, and they shunned open discussion with the other side.

The wranglings of the two sides were given a superficial resolution by imperial interference. The emperors, ever since Constantine recognized the Christian religion, had tried to keep the doctrinal peace. In 410 the emperor Honorius sent his high functionary Count Marcellinus to impose religious uniformity in Africa. When early attempts at this failed, Marcellinus called a "Confrontation" (*collatio*) where Catholics and Donatists argued their respective causes. For this solemn occasion, 284 Donatist bishops and 286 Catholic bishops showed up, having been guaranteed safe travel to and from Carthage by Marcellinus. The Donatists, who lost this great debate, complained that Marcellinus was a biased judge. But Paul Monceaux disagrees, and Peter Brown sides with him (B 322).[1] Manceaux wrote of Marcellinus: "Patient under every test, he moderated the debates with authority, never rude, but also never weak, with a lawyerly respect for everyone's rights."[2] W. H. C. Frend, the sympathetic historian of Donatism, says that the Donatists did not make a good case for themselves:

In contrast to the Catholics, who leave the impression of abiding by a well-thought-out scheme of attack, the Donatists prepared their case indifferently. They even included documents which could help their opponents and, as already mentioned, they seem to have been unable to decide until the last moment whether to include their primate [Primian] among the delegates chosen for debate. Perhaps they felt that Primian was too vulnerable on the Maximianist issue [as the suppressor of another religious body]—perhaps there were other grounds [like old age].[3]

The Catholic case was pressed home mainly by three bishops—Augustine, his lawyer friend Alypius, and the bishop of Carthage, Aurelius. Monceaux describes the proceedings:

> There is enjoyment to be found in the plot-twists of this imposing pageant—in the strategies, for instance, of either side, the clear and concerted plan of the Catholics, the inventiveness of the Donatist obstructers. Above all, the mobile features are limned of some great orators. In the schismatic ranks, the headlong Petilian of Constantine, imaginative, rasping, unbending, slippery, almost always eloquent—or Emeritus of Caesarea, unbending too, but high-minded, often wordy and drawn-out, but at times sparkling and witty. On the Catholic side, in a circle of outstanding speakers, all of them his friends, the clear winner of the Confrontation was Augustine, the verbal technician of his age, impassioned, wary, discriminating, and deadly.[4]

Marcellinus found for the Catholics and ordered the Donatists to give up their churches and join the Catholics. This was easier to declare than to enforce (B 309–16, 335–36). Frend claims: "In the countryside, archaeologists have yet to find clear evidence for the transformation of a Donatist church into a Catholic one."[5] But, insofar as it was justified, Augustine had to come up with a rationale for this suppression of religious freedom. He offered to share his own basilica with the Donatist bishop of Hippo. He told the Catholics not to crow over vanquished Donatists (*Epistulae* 78.8). When Donatists murdered two of his priests, he asked the authorities not to execute, maim, or flog the men—they should live on, to repent (*Epistulae* 133.1).

In his most famous defense of legal coercion, he argued that habit had blinded the Donatists to the truth, and they had to be forcibly brought before the teachers they had ignored. Once again he invoked the Donatists' own Tyconius, who said the Jewish Law was like a pedagogue who forced children to school—it made them listen to the Lord. He invoked Jesus's parable of the wedding banquet—when the invited guests do not show up, people are sent into the hedge and byways with the order: "Compel them to come in." Augustine used both verbs available to him in the Gospel of Luke—*coge intrare* (in the African text) and *compelle intrare* (in the Roman).

> Let the heretics be drawn from the hedges, be extracted from the thorns. Stuck in the hedges, they do not want to be compelled [*cogi*]: "We will enter when we want to." But that is not the Lord's command; He said, "Compel them to come in." Use compulsion on the outside, so freedom can arise once they are inside. (*Sermones* 112.8)

Augustine was never entirely comfortable with this line. For one thing, he worried about *ficti*, false converts going along to escape the law without really learning the truth (B 269). He also feared vindictiveness in the Catholic enforcers. When Marcellinus was imprisoned after an attempted coup, Augustine pleaded for his life, unsuccessfully. After his execution Brown sees in Augustine a turn against the compulsions of the law:

> At this crucial moment, Augustine showed that he was no Ambrose: he lacked the streak of obstinacy and confidence that he could control events that is so marked in the great ecclesiastical politicians of his age. . . . The incident also marks, on a deeper level, the end of a period of Augustine's

life. For, paradoxically, he had lost his enthusiasm for the alliance between the Roman Empire and the Catholic Church at just the time when it had become effectively cemented. The alliance remained as a practical necessity, a *sine qua non* of the organized life of his church; it would be invoked against other heretics, the Pelagians; but there is little trace, now, of the heady confidence of the 400's. For now that he no longer needed to convince others, Augustine seems to have lost conviction himself; he fell back on more somber views.[6]

So, even though he had been brought to an Ambrosian view of the usefulness of church coercion, he had none of the scourge-wielding swagger of the Milanese strong man. With the second and third ways in which he came around to Ambrose—reliance on miracles and his usefulness against the Pelagians—he became more comfortable.

On the second matter, that of miracles, it was noted earlier that he was skeptical of modern miracles during his time in Milan and for a while after— a position for which he expressed regret in his *Retractiones*.[7] The Donatist cult of martyrs and of miracles worked by their relics, led to a flourishing trade in relics, so much so that Augustine wrote, "As for Africa, is it not filled with the bodies of holy martyrs?" (*Epistulae* 78.3). The scramble to have patron relics in every little spot led a synod meeting in Carthage in 401 to demand stricter authentication of true relics.[8] Since there were so many saints to be celebrated, Augustine complained that observing each feast day would grow tedious and blunt the piety of the people.[9]

Nonetheless, devotion to martyr relics, from which miracles were expected, was so woven into the religious life of Africans, and was so much an advantage of the Donatist shrines, that Augustine was soon imitating Ambrose's cult of martyr miracles. In a famous chapter of *The City of God* (22.8), he describes twenty-six miracles worked by relics of which he claimed personal knowledge. Twelve of these were performed by the relics of the first martyr Stephen, whose chapel beside Augustine's own basilica was as important to him as Gervase and Protase had been to Ambrose. In 415 the supposed grave of Stephen was found in Gaza, to great acclaim. Soon dust from his body and small bone splinters were carried throughout Christendom. Augustine's friend and follower Orosius brought some of the dust to Hippo, where a chapel was built for it.[10]

We have nine sermons Augustine preached on Saint Stephen, including the one with which he dedicated the chapel built for the relic in 424. As usual, he emphasized that the saint should be *honored* there, but only God should be *worshiped* there (*Sermones* 218.3). Augustine opposed superstitious ways of asking for temporal benefits from the saints:

> The martyr Stephen, blessed as the first after the apostles to be appointed deacon by the apostles, yet crowned [with martyrdom] before the apostles, shed glory on a far land by his suffering, and has come to visit us after his death. What a small amount of dust to gather so many people here! The dust is not visible [in its container] but the favor bestowed is manifest. Consider, my dear ones, what God has in store for us in the region of life when he gives us such honor in the dust of the dead. The flesh of Stephen is famous in many places, but it is the merit of his faith that is committed to us. Let our hope to receive temporal benefits be such that we merit eternal benefits by imitating him. To heed, to believe, to act on what he gives us to imitate by his suffering—that is the true honoring of a martyr. (*Sermones* 317.1)

On the third point of resort to Ambrose, it is important to consider his fight with Pelagians, especially with Caelestius and Julian of Eclanum. Asserting the reality of original sin derived from Adam, he began to use Ambrose as his trump card. He asked Ambrose's former secretary Paulinus to write up memories of the man, to confirm his saintly authority. Then, in the *Contra Julianum, Opus Imperfectum,* the name of Ambrose tolls like a bell throughout the text—about 120 citations of him occur in that work. He was betting that Julian would not dare attack the venerated Ambrose, and his gamble paid off.

Ambrose's words forcefully contradicted Mani. For Mani said that our nature is tainted with a foreign substance of evil, while *Ambrose* said that our nature is crippled by the defection of the first man. On the subject we are now debating, *Ambrose* said that Christ's flesh was conceived free of sin, separating it from all other human births—entirely at odds with what Mani said.[11] What *Ambrose* believes, I believe, and Mani believes with neither of us. Why then do you keep trying to set me apart from *Ambrose* and link me with Mani? If Mani taught that original sin did not come from the taint of a foreign substance but was part of our own nature crippled at birth, both *Ambrose* and I would agree. Would you then lump us *both* with him? But if that is not the teaching of Mani (and surely it is not), and I agree with *Ambrose*, why do you deny that we differ from him? You keep asking why I claim alliance with the bishop of Milan, and you try in vain to separate me from him. How can you maintain that only because I have no shield, I seek for medicine from him? Whether you like it or not, Christ is the shield both for me and for *Ambrose*, and *Ambrose* is my medicine only because he heals the wounds you inflict— and not only does he, but so do Cyprian and Hilary, and other men like them whose catholic belief you lash out at. So do not be upset that *Ambrose*, Cyprian, and Hilary are a medicine for the wounds you inflict, though you are forced to see how slight are the medicines Pelagius and Caelestius and whoever else can bring to your own damnation.

I can call *Ambrose* to witness for the Catholic faith against the Manicheans, while all you have to offer the Manicheans is medicine for their wounds or, worse, assistance in their error. For the Manicheans say that evil is a thing in itself, a reality as eternal as the good created by God, since they think that evil cannot have come from good. But *Ambrose* refuted that, saying "Evil can arise from good things, not because they are evil in themselves but because they lack some good. The source of evil is simply a lack of the good."[12] How do you answer this? You say, with the Manicheans, "Nature does not permit evil to arise from good, or justice from criminality." Such words side with the Manicheans against *Ambrose*, and they come from the famous four books in which you tried to answer my single volume. If you were a judge between the two, you would have to give your verdict for the Manicheans against *Ambrose*. And this would not embarrass you, since you slander those you criticize [Augustine], praise those you inadvertently criticize [*Ambrose*], and help those [Manicheans] you use to criticize others.[13]

Julian argued that Augustine was still a Manichean in his belief that there had been a fall of man that left him with a tendency toward sin; that Augustine condemned sex and marriage, which is an insult to the good creator; and that his own past, described in *Confessions*, poisoned his view of human nature and made him deny the power of free will to stay free of sin. The differences between the men were temperamental as well as theological. Julian was a cheerful ascetic who stayed celibate with ease and thought everyone could do the same. Augustine proved that Ambrose believed in original sin. He was even willing to use the postbaptismal washing of the feet to cancel the effect of the serpent's bite on Adam's foot. Though Augustine did not himself use that rite, he said that it proved Ambrose's belief in original sin.[14] As Peter Brown says, "Julian, significantly, skirts round Augustine's citations from Ambrose."[15]

Thus, in the long and complex story of Augustine's fraught relationship with Ambrose, the younger man had ample years to reassess and appropriate what he needed from the figure he at first dismissed as too worldly and demagogic. Ambrose, after all, died before he was sixty, after only twenty years as bishop (a brief span for so many achievements). Augustine was seventy-six when he died, after thirty-four years as bishop. Dragged into an active life from the serene retirement he wanted so achingly, the African contemplative had to go back to school to the Roman senator of ecclesiology. In some ways this experience hardened him. But it also humbled him. After resisting his school teachers as a boy, he found it necessary to seek out a guide in his old age. As usual, the tougher Ambrose prevailed.

The story of Ambrose and Augustine is a tangled one, full of surprises. The tale becomes even more amazing when their contemporary Jerome is joined with the other two to make up the core of the church's "Western fathers." James O'Donnell rightly sums up the odd situation:

> It is amazing, in retrospect, how much the team of Ambrose, Augustine, and Jerome count for when in real life they formed such a fragile triangle, Jerome on the outs with both of them, Augustine nearly bailing on Ambrose, Ambrose not really having a sense of what he was dealing with when he looked at the other two. It is like one of those big league clubhouses where the manager, the slugger, and the big right-hander can't stand each other, but they go out and win the World Series anyway.[16]

By luck or providence they helped one another transcend their individual shortcomings and became stronger together than any of them could have been standing alone.

Notes

Introduction

1. Mario Mirabella Roberti, "La cattedrale antica di Milano e il suo Battistero," *Arte Lombarda* 8 (1963): 77–98; Mirabella Roberti, *Milano Romana* (Rusconi Immagini, 1984), 106–11; Dale Kinney, "Le chiese paleocristiane di Mediolanum," in *Milano, una capitale da Ambrogio ai Carolingi*, ed. Carlo Bertelli (Electa, 1987), 48–60.
2. Richard Krautheimer, *Three Christian Capitals: Topography and Politics* (University of California Press, 1983), 76.
3. Mirabella Roberti, "La cattedrale," 80–86.
4. Attilio Pracchi, *La cattedrale antica di Milano: Il problema delle chiese doppie fra tarda antichità e medioevo* (Laterza, 1996), 8–23.
5. Ambrose, *Explanatio Symboli* 1 (*CSEL* 82.7): "The holy work [*mysteria*] of the inspections has been performed. It was ascertained that no taint adhered to anyone's body. By this exorcism it was sought and insured that not only the body but the soul is made sacred."
6. Ibid., "semper presens custodia, certe thesaurus pectoris nostri."

7. Mirabella Roberti, "La cattedrale," 86–90, contains a careful attempt to imagine the interior of the baptistry.

8. Ambrose, *Letters* 26.8.

9. Ambrose, *Letters* 44.4.

10. Ambrose, *Exaemeron* 1.13 (*CSEL* 32.1).

11. Mirabella Roberti, *Arte Lombarda*, 88–90, Kinney, "Le chiese paleocristiane," 53–54.

12. Silvia Lusuardi Siena, ed., *Piazza Duomo prima del Duomo* (Veneranda Fabbrica del Duomo di Milano, 2009), 12.

13. It was once thought (and some still think) that Ambrose must have built the baptistry at the same time that he composed the poem for its dedication. But he could have added it at any time, and the whole double cathedral complex seems to antedate his bishopric.

14. Ernesto Brivio, *The Duomo*, 2nd ed. (Veneranda Fabbrica del Duomo di Milano, 2002).

Chapter 1

1. Cesare Alzati, *Ambrosianum Mysterium: The Church of Milan and its Liturgical Tradition*, trans. George Guiver, 2 vols. (Grove Books, 1999–2000).

2. Ibid., 1:77.

3. Dario Fo, *Sant' Ambrogio e l'invenzione di Milano* (Einaudi, 2009), 3.

4. J. H. W. G. Liebeschuetz, *Ambrose of Milan: Political Letters and Speeches* (Liverpool University Press, 2005), 25, 39.

5. Edward Gibbon, *The Decline and Fall of the Roman Empire*, chapter 27.

6. Cosima Wagner, who read from Gibbon night after night to her husband, wrote in her diary: "We cannot get over our astonishment that dramatists do not go for their material to Gibbon . . . the episode of Ambrose and Theodosius . . . tremendously interesting conflicts involving human beings." *Cosima Wagner's Diaries*, translated by Geoffrey Skelton, vol. 1, *1869–1877* (Harcourt, Brace, Jovanovich, 1978), 507.

7. On San Simpliciano see: Mario Mirabella Roberti, *Milano Romana* (Rusconi Immagini, 1984), 132–36; Richard Krautheimer, *Three Christian Capitals: Topography and Politics* (University of California Press, 1983), 74, 81; Richard Krautheimer and Slobodan Ćurčić, *Early Christian and Byzantine Architecture*, 4th ed. (Yale University Press, 1986), 82–83, 175; Josef Schmitz, *Gottesdienst im altchristlichen Mailand*

(Peter Hanstein Verlag, 1975), 270–72; Maria Teresa Fiorio, ed., *Le chiese di Milano*, rev. ed. (Electa, 2006), 156–62.

8. On San Nazaro see: Mirabella Roberti, *Milano Romana*, 125–29; Krautheimer, *Three Christian Capitals*, 74, 80; Krautheimer and Ćurčić, *Early Christian and Byzantine Architecture*, 74, 80; Schmitz, *Gottesdienst*, 262–68; Fiorio, *Le chiese di Milano*, 344–46.

9. On San Lorenzo see: Mirabella Roberti, *Milano Romana*, 137–56; Krautheimer, *Three Christian Capitals*, 81–92; Krautheimer and Ćurčić, *Early Christian and Byzantine Architecture*, 79–81; Schmitz, *Gottesdienst*, 257–59; Fiorio, *Le chiese di Milano*, 416–20.

10. On Sant'Ambrogio see: Mirabella Roberti, *Milano Romana*, 120–29; Krautheimer, *Three Christian Capitals*, 74, 79; Krautheimer and Ćurčić, *Early Christian and Byzantine Architecture*, 174–75; Schmitz, *Gottesdienst*, 268–70; Fiorio, *Le chiese di Milano*, 57–61.

11. Some, like Krautheimer, doubt that San Dionigi, which was partly demolished in 1549 and its last traces destroyed in 1783, dates back to Ambrose, but Mirabella Roberti, the dean of Milan archeologists, argues for its authenticity (*Milano Romana*, 130–31). So do Josef Schmitz, *Gottesdienst*, 262; E. Cattaneo, "San Dionigi basilica paleocristiana?" *Archivio Ambrosiano* 27 (1973–1974): 72–73; Gino Traversi, "Una nota su San Dionigi, basilica ambrosiana sconosciuta," *Arte Lombarda* 8 (1963): 99–102; and Fiorio, *Le chiese di Milano*, 183.

12. This spelling is used instead of the more familiar Latinized "Monica," since it reflects its Berber origins (it is likely derived from the North African goddess Mon) and thus Monnica's Donatist background (Berber names were prevalent among Donatists).

13. Peter Brown, *The Cult of the Saints: Its Rise and Function in Latin Christianity* (University of Chicago Press, 1981), 44.

14. For the power—social, political, and economic—of the desert ascetics in the fourth and fifth centuries, see Peter Brown, "The Rise and Function of the Holy Man in Late Antiquity," *Journal of Roman Studies* 66 (1971): 80–101. For Athanasius's response to this threat, see David Brakke, *Athanasius and the Politics of Asceticism* (Oxford University Press, 1995), 65–66, 99–141, 213–14.

15. Peter Brown, "The Very Special Dead," in Brown, *Cult of the Saints*, 69–85.

16. For a list of martyr relics and their sites in North Italy, see Mark Humphries, *Communities of the Blessed: Social environment and religious change in northern Italy, AD 200–400* (Oxford University Press, 1999), 221–27.

17. Ammianus Marcellinus, *Res Gestae* 27.7.5.6.

18. See Neil McLynn, "The Transformation of Imperial Churchgoing in the Fourth Century," in *Approaching Late Antiquity: The Transformation from Early to Late Empire*, ed. Simon Swain and Mark Edwards (Oxford University Press, 2004), 246–48, 266.

19. Brown, *Cult of the Saints*, 37.

20. Ibid., 141–48, for the processional culture of the fourth century.

21. Ambrose, *De Excessu Fratris*.

22. Krautheimer, *Three Christian Capitals*, 83–88, W. Eugene Kleinbauer, "Toward a Dating of San Lorenzo in Milan: Masonry and Building Methods of Milanese and Early Christian Architecture," *Arte Lombarda* 13, no. 2 (1968): 1–22.

23. Aristide Calderini, Gino Chierici, and Carlo Cecchelli, *La Basilica di San Lorenzo Maggiore in Milano* (Bocca, 1951), 85–120.

24. Mirabella Roberti, *Milano Romana*, 146–51.

25. Gian Alberto Dell'Acqua, ed., *La basilica di San Lorenzo in Milano* (Banco Populare di Milano, 1985), 19–21. As a basilica outside the city walls, the church would need defenses of its own at a time when the Visigoth Alaric was threatening northern Italy. On the other hand, if this is the time when the church was first built, why place it in the path of danger?

26. Laura Fieni, ed., *La costruzione della Basilica San Lorenzo a Milano* (Silvana Editoriale, 2004), 71–90. More precisely, she dates the bricks from wood survivals in their firing (253–55), which are hard to fix within a decade or so. She too believes the four towers had a military purpose. But towers at a fort are meant to protect the curtain wall that keeps invaders out, and there is no archeological evidence that there were ever such walls at the Basilica Portiana. She explains this by supposing that Stilicho had to leave the site before he completed it.

27. Kleinbauer, "Toward a Dating of San Lorenzo."

28. Ausonius, *Ordo Urbium Nobilium*, verse 5.

29. Dale Kinney, "The Evidence for the Dating of S. Lorenzo in Milan," *Journal of the Society of Architectural Historians* 31 (1972): 92–107.

30. Krautheimer, *Three Christian Capitals*, 83.

31. Mirabella Roberti, *Milano Romana*, 140, quoting *The Life of Saint Veranius*.

32. After an earthquake toppled the central dome in 1523, Milan's archbishop Charles Borromeo ordered his favored architect, Pellegrino Tibaldi, to retain as much of the original plan as possible, out of respect for the church's historical importance (Fiorio, *Le chiese di Milano*, 407–10).

33. Ambrose, *De Excessu Fratris* 30–32.

34. It is a dream in *Confessions* (9.7) but a vision after Augustine became more devoted to Ambrose (*City of God* 22.8). Ambrose does not specify what "telling clues" (signa convenientia, Letter 77.1) led him to the remains. See Francesco Scorza Barcellona, "L'invenzione dell reliquie dei martiri Protasio e Gervasio," in *387 D.C.: Ambrogio e Agostino; Le sorgenti dell'Europa*, ed. Paolo Pasini (Olivares, 2003), 211–14.

35. Mirabella Roberti, *Milano Romana*, 120. The frontal has a side toward the congregation worked all in gold by Volvinius's assistant, showing in relief episodes from the life of Christ. The other side, toward the clergy, is worked in silver and gold by Volvinius himself, and it shows episodes from the life of Ambrose, pairing them with the gospel mysteries and making Ambrose a "second Christ." In the middle panel Christ crowns both Angilbert and Volvinius. On the sides are representations of Milan's patron martyrs. See Sandrina Bandera, *L'altare d'oro di Ambrogio* 4th ed. (Sady Francinetti, 2006).

36. Eusebius, *Life of Constantine* 1.28–291.

37. Suzanne Lewis, "The Latin Iconography of the Single-Naved Cruciform Basilica Apostolorum in Milan," *Art Bulletin* 51 (1969): 205–19.

38. Krautheimer and Ćurčić, *Early Christian and Byzantine Architecture*, 182.

39. Krautheimer, *Three Christian Capitals*, 81.

40. Attilio Pracchi, *La cattedrale antica di Milano: Il problema delle chiese doppie fra tarda antichità e medioevo* (Laterza, 1996), 8–23.

41. Ibid., 58.

Chapter 2

1. For the gendered training of classical statesmen, see Maud W. Gleason, *Making Men: Sophists and Self-Presentation in Ancient Rome* (Princeton University Press, 1995).

2. Peter Brown, *Power and Persuasion in Late Antiquity: Towards a Christian Empire* (University of Wisconsin Press, 1992), 57.

3. Ibid., 56. Cf. Peter Brown, *The Body and Society: Men, Women, and Sexual Renunciation in Early Christianity* (Columbia University Press, 1988), 10–12. And note 49: "Ever since the second century, *eutaxia, euschēmosynē, semnotes*—terms that conjured up the ideal of a self-controlled, even awesome, bearing—were those most current on grave inscriptions and in laudatory accounts of leading citizens."

4. Ibid., 111–13.

5. For Latin *officium* as the Stoics' Greek *kathēkon*, see Ivor Davidson's introduction to his edition and translation of *De Officiis* (Oxford University Press), 1.

6. John Matthews, *Western Aristocracies and Imperial Court, A.D. 364–425* (Clarendon, 1975), 186.

7. Gait (*gressus*) was particularly important, as we see from the anonymous fourth-century *De Physiognomia*: "When hands and feet are made to move in rhythm with the rest of a man's body, and his shoulders are carried with a quiet control of a supple neck, the man is called large in spirit and courageous, for this is the tread of a lion." *Traité de physiognomonie*, ed. Jacques André (Belles Lettres, 1981), 76.

8. Neil B. McLynn, *Ambrose of Milan: Church and Court in a Christian Capital* (University of California Press, 1994), 32–33.

9. Brown, *Power and Persuasion*, 76.

10. Brown, *Body and Society*, 346–47.

11. Ibid., 342–45.

12. Ibid., 346.

13. Matthews, *Western Aristocracies and Imperial Court*, 196.

14. Claudian, *Panegyricus Probino et Olybrio* 43–44.

15. Ammianus Marcellinus, *Res Gestae* 27.11.

16. Ibid., 30.9.5

17. Dudden, *The Life and Times of Saint Ambrose*, 2 vols. (Clarendon, 1935), Palanque, *Saint Ambroise et l'Empire Romain: Contribution à l'histoire des rapports de l'église et de l'état à la fin du quatrième siècle* (Boccard, 1933), Paredi, *S. Ambrogio e la sua eta*, 2nd ed. (Hoepli, 1960).

18. Some leading Ambrosian revisionists, listed in chronological order, are: Roger Gryson, *Scolies Ariennes sur le Concile d'Aquilée* (Editions du Cerf, 1980); R. P. C. Hanson, *The Search for the Christian Doctrine of God: The Arian Controversy, 318–381* (Clark, 1988); McLynn, *Ambrose of Milan* (1994); Daniel H. Williams, *Ambrose of Milan and the End of the Nicene-Arian Conflicts* (Oxford University Press, 1995); John Moorhead, *Ambrose: Church and Society in the Late Roman World* (Longman, 1999); Ivor J. Davidson, ed. and trans., *De Officiis* (Oxford University Press, 2001); J. H. W. G. Liebeschuetz, ed. and trans., *Ambrose of Milan: Political Letters and Speeches* (Liverpool University Press, 2005); Alan Cameron, *The Last Pagans of Rome* (Oxford University Press, 2010).

19. Williams, *Ambrose of Milan*, 121–27.

20. Ibid., 76–83, on the opposition to Auxentius.

21. Brown, *Power and Persuasion*, 96.

22. For the scholia to *De Fide* of Palladius of Ratiaria, see Gryson, *Scolies Ariennes*, 264–74.

23. Hanson, *Search for the Christian Doctrine*, 669.

24. For the Arian scholia to the acta of the council, see Gryson, *Scolies Ariennes*, 204–34.

25. Ibid., 226.

26. Ibid., 300, on Ambrose's *lascivi sordidique anni*.

Chapter 3

1. I follow the careful chronology for these confusing events as charted by J. H. W. G. Liebeschuetz in *Ambrose of Milan: Political Letters and Speeches* (Liverpool University Press, 2005), 124–45.

2. Consider the embarrassment of Emperor Valens when he tried to attend churches of the East with their resisting bishops: Neil B. McLynn, "The Transformation of Imperial Churchgoing in the Fourth Century," in *Approaching Late Antiquity: The Transformation from Early to Late Empire*, ed. Simon Swain and Mark Edwards (Oxford University Press, 2004), 253–56.

3. See Sozomen, *Historia Ecclesiastica* 7.13 on "this cruel law," and Rufinus, *Historia Ecclesiastica* 2.16.

4. McLynn, "Imperial Churchgoing," 251–70.

5. Neil B. McLynn, *Ambrose of Milan* (University of California Press, 1994), 197.

6. Peter Brown, *The Rise of Western Christendom: Triumph and Diversity, A.D. 200–1000*, 2nd ed. (Blackwell, 2003), 15–16, 458.

Chapter 4

1. Neil B. McLynn, *Ambrose of Milan* (University of California Press, 1994), 266.

2. Ibid., 151–53, 312–13, 145–46.

3. Symmachus's *Relatio Tertia* is preserved in the correspondence of Ambrose as Letter 72a (*CSEL* 10.3).

Chapter 5

1. Augustine, *Soliloquia* 2.26.
2. Pierre Courcelle, *Recherches sur les Confessions de Saint Augustin* (Boccard, 1950), 93–138.
3. Claudian, *Panegyricus Dictus Manlio Theodoro Consuli*, 94, 149–50.
4. Ibid., 84–86. The poet devotes seventy-four lines of his 360-line tribute to Theodore's scholarly retreat from active politics.
5. Claudian, too, praises Theodore for teaching "what way one takes to happiness" (*Panegyricus* 94–95).
6. Augustine, *De Beata Vita* 1.4–5.
7. Gennadius, *Scriptores Ecclesiastici*, 36.
8. Ambrose, *Epistulae* 2 (CSEL 82, part 1).
9. Augustine, *De Civitate Dei* 10.29.
10. Cicero, *Hortensius*, ed. Alberto Grilli (Istituto Editorale Cisalpine, 1962), 52.
11. Augustine, *De Ordine* 2.2.7 and *De Vera Religion* 47.
12. Augustine, *Epistulae* 2.

Chapter 6

1. He also blamed her for not arranging an early marriage for him (C 2.3). Monnica was waiting for Augustine to reach a social status that would involve marriage to an heiress (C 6.25). He said that his mother had fled the center of the earthly Babylon "but still lingered on its outskirts" (C 2.8).
2. Ambrose, *De Elias t Jejunio* 78–81 (CSEL 32.2).
3. Later, in places like Rome, there could be as many as seven exorcisms in the course of the Lenten preparation for baptism, but in Milan and most places during the fourth century there seem to have been only three. Josef Schmitz, *Gottesdienst im altchristlichen Mailand* (Peter Hanstein Verlag, 1975), 69.
4. Ambrose, *Explanatio Symboli* 1.
5. Eusebius, *Historia Ecclesiastica* 6.43.11.
6. Peter Brown, *The Rise of Western Christendom: Triumph and Diversity A.D. 200–1000*, 2nd ed. (Blackwell, 2003), 66.
7. Ambrose, *Expositio in Lucam* 4.76.

8. Ambrose, *De Elia et Jejunio* 3 (*CSEL* 32.2).

9. Ibid., 22.

10. Ibid., 34.

11. Ibid., 84–85.

12. Ambrose, *De Joseph* 1.1 (*CSEL* 32.2).

13. On the date of the treatises, see Marcia L. Colish, *Ambrose's Patriarchs: Ethics for the Common Man* (University of Notre Dame Press, 2005), 24–28.

14. Ambrose, *De Abraham* (*CSEL* 32.1).

15. Colish, *Ambrose's Patriarchs*, 31–40.

16. Ambrose, *De Isaac* (*CSEL* 32.1).

17. Ambrose, *De Jacob* (*CSEL* 32.2).

18. Augustine, *De Diversis Quaestionaibus ad Simplcianum* 3.

19. Colish, *Ambrose's Patriarchs*, 24–25.

20. Ambrose, *De Excessu Fratris* 38–39 (*CSEL* 73.7).

21. Ibid. 41.

22. Ambrose, *De Joseph* (*CSEL* 32.2).

23. Paula Fredriksen, *Augustine and the Jews: A Christian Defense of Jews and Judaism* (Doubleday, 2008).

24. Ibid., 241.

25. Suzanne Poque, "Les lectures liturgiques de l'Octave pascale à Hippone d'après les traités de saint Augustin sur la permière epître de S. Jean," *Revue Benedictine* 74 (1964): 217–41.

Chapter 7

1. Ambrose, *Explanatio Symboli* 3 (*CSEL* 73.7).

2. Donald J. Mastronarde, ed., *Medea* (Cambridge University Press, 2002), 271.

3. On the seasonal rotation in double cathedrals, see Attilio Pracchi, *La cattedrale antica di Milano: Il problema delle chiese doppie fra tarda antichità e medioevo* (Laterza, 1996), 8–23.

4. Ibid., 7–8, for possible use of both baptistries in Milan. See *The City of God* 22.8 for women coming out of a separate baptistry.

5. Public baths seem to have had separate sectors for men and women, though mixed bathing was also allowed. See Garrett G. Fagan, *Bathing in Public in the Roman World* (University of Michigan Press, 1999), 24–29.

6. Peter Brown, *The Body and Society: Men, Women, and Sexual Renunciation in Early Christianity* (Columbia University Press, 1988), 315.
7. Pier Franco Beatrice, *La lavanda dei piedi: Contributo alla storia delle antiche liturgie cristiane* (CLV Edizioni Liturgiche, 1983), 114–20.
8. Craig Alan Satterlee, *Ambrose of Milan's Method of Mystagogical Preaching* (Liturgical Press, 2002), 180.

Chapter 8

1. *Sacramenta* did not mean the seven sacraments of later church history. The Latin word was used for oaths (military or otherwise), the ceremony of oath taking, or the body one was initiated into by oath. Ambrose used it for the bonds that were formed by the ceremony of baptism.
2. Suzanne Poque, "Les lectures liturgiques de l'Octave pascale à Hippone d'après les traités de saint Augustin sur la première epître de S. Jean," *Revue Benedictine* 74 (1964): 224–25.
3. Craig Alan Satterlee, *Ambrose of Milan's Method of Mystagogical Preaching* (Liturgical Press, 2002).

Chapter 9

1. For Augustine's sacramental minimalism, see Maxwell E. Johnson, *The Rites of Christian Initiation: Their Evolution and Interpretation*, rev. ed. (Liturgical Press, 2007), 188, 197–98.
2. W. H. C. Frend, *The Rise of Christianity* (Fortress, 1984), 655–56.
3. Augustine, *Enarrationes in Psalmos* (CSEL 94/1), on Ps. 95.11.
4. Augustine, *Psalmus contra Partem Donati* (CSEL 51).
5. Augustine, *De Baptismo* 2.1.2, 6.2.3 (CSEL 51).
6. Ibid., 5.17.22.
7. Ibid., 7.53.102.
8. Ibid., 1.13.21.
9. Ibid., 4.24.32.
10. Ibid., 5.7.8
11. For Augustine's use of classical allusion against Julian, see Garry Wills, "Vergil and St. Augustine," in *A Companion to Vergil's Aeneid and Its*

Tradition, ed. Joseph Farrell and Michael C. J. Putnam (Wiley-Blackwell, 2010), 128–29, 131–32.

Chapter 10

1. It was called Hippo Regius (Royal Hippo) because Numidian kings were supposed to have lived there in the distant past.
2. Erwan Marec, *Monuments chrétiens d'Hippone: Ville épiscopale de saint Augustin* (Arts et Métiers Graphiques, 1958); Frederik van der Meer, *Augustine the Bishop: The Life and Work of a Father of the Church*, trans. Brian Battershaw and G. R. Lamb (Sheed & Ward, 1961), 17–23; William Harmless, "Baptism," in *Augustine through the Ages: An Encyclopedia*, ed. Allan D. Fitzgerald (Eerdmans, 1999), 83–91.
3. Van der Meer, *Augustine the Bishop*, 22.
4. Marec, *Monuments chrétiens*, 110–12.
5. Cyril of Jerusalem, *Katecheseis Mystagogikai* 1.1.
6. William Harmless, *Augustine and the Catechumenate* (Liturgical Press, 1995), 69. Everett Ferguson, *Baptism in the Early Church: History, Theology, and Liturgy in the First Five Centuries* (Eerdmans, 2009), 67–84.
7. For the Lord's Prayer as a "washing" of postbaptismal sin, compare Sermon 213.9.
8. Augustine, *In Johannis Evangelium Tractatus* 11.3.
9. Augustine, *Epistulae* 24.6, 31.9, 32.3.
10. Augustine, *De Baptismo* 3.16.21. Sermon 324.
11. Augustine, *The City of God* 22.8.

Chapter 11

1. Peter Brown, *Augustine of Hippo: A Biography*, rev. ed. (University of California Press, 2000), 290.
2. Paul Monceaux, *Histoire littéraire de l'Afrique chrétienne depuis les origins jusqu'à l'invasion arabe*, vol. 4 (Leroux, 1912), 112.
3. W. H. C. Frend, *The Donatist Church: A Movement of Protest in Roman North Africa* (Clarendon, 1952), 279.
4. Monceaux, *Histoire littéraire*, 425.
5. Frend, *The Donatist Church*, 299.

6. Brown, *Augustine of Hippo*, 337–38.

7. Augustine, *Retractationes* 1.13, 7.

8. Frederik van der Meer, *Augustine the Bishop: The Life and Work of a Father of the Church*, trans. Brian Battershaw and G. R. Lamb (Sheed & Ward, 1961), 483.

9. Ibid., 482.

10. Ibid., 475–76.

11. Ambrose, *Expositio Evangelii Secundum Lucan* 405 (*CCL* 14).

12. Ambrose, *De Isaac* 7 (*CSEL* 32.1).

13. Augustine, *Contra Julianum, Opus Imperfectum* 4.109 (*PL* 45), emphasis added.

14. Ibid., 1.71.

15. Brown, *Augustine of Hippo*, 388.

16. James O'Donnell, personal correspondence; cited with permission.

Index

INDEX